Reading

The Day the Mountain Moved

Caroline Banks
Tom Rowe

Illustrated by Nicholas Read

PRENTICE HALL REGENTS
Englewood Cliffs, New Jersey 07632

Library of Congress Cataloging-in-Publication Data

Banks, Caroline
    The day the mountain moved / Caroline Banks, Tom Rowe:
illustrated by Nicholas Read.
        p.   cm. — (Readings in English: 1)
    ISBN 0-13-199845-5
    1. English language—Textbooks for foreign speakers. 2.
College readers. I. Rowe, Tom. (date) II. Title.   III. Series: Banks,
Caroline. Readings in English: 1.
PE1128.B2993   1990
428.6'4—dc20   89-26616
                                                        CIP

Editorial production
and supervision: *Shirley Hinkamp*
Interior design: *LMD Service to Publishers*
Cover Design: *Diane Saxe*
Manufacturing buyer: *Ray Keating*

©1990 by Prentice-Hall, Inc.
A division of Simon & Schuster
Englewood Cliffs, New Jersey 07632

Printed in the United States of America
10 9 8 7 6 5 4 3 2 1

ISBN 0-13-199845-5

Prentice-Hall International (UK) Limited, *London*
Prentice-Hall of Australia Pty. Limited, *Sydney*
Prentice-Hall Canada Inc., *Toronto*
Prentice-Hall Hispanoamericana, S.A., *Mexico*
Prentice-Hall of India Private Limited, *New Delhi*
Prentice-Hall of Japan, Inc., *Tokyo*
Simon & Schuster Asia Pte., Ltd., *Singapore*
Editora Prentice-Hall do Brasil, Ltda., *Rio de Janeiro*

ACKNOWLEDGMENTS

The authors are grateful to:

Simon & Schuster and International Creative Man-
agement for permission to reprint the extract from
Teacher by Sylvia Ashton-Warner. Copyright 1963
by Sylvia Ashton-Warner.

The Boston Herald for News stories and photos
about the Blizzard of 1978. February 5–8, 1978.

Florence Alexander and the estate of Marilyn Hirsh
for *The Elephants and the Mice.* Copyright 1970 by
Marilyn Hirsh.

We also thank the publishers for:

"Anansi and the Plantains" from *Anansi the Spider Man and Other Stories* by Philip Sherlock, etc.
Reprinted by permission of Harper & Row, Publishers.

"I Know an Old Lady" by Alan Mills and Rose
Bonne. Copyright 1952, 1960 by Peer International
(Canada) Ltd. International rights secured. All
rights reserved. Used by permission.

Thanks to Paul LaRose for "A Letter to Debbie."

Special thanks to Paul Hannigan and Anne Read
for all their help and love.

Contents

Part Four   Disaster!   77

The weather can be violent, and the earth can move suddenly.
Things can go wrong. Sometimes it's serious, sometimes not.

Part Five   Tell Me a Story   101

Once upon a time: Stories from around the world

Indexes

To the Student

We wrote this book for you and we've included texts of many types—stories, articles, poems, and songs—from many parts of the English-speaking world.

The book begins with stories written in language that will probably be familiar to you, and gradually it uses more new vocabulary. The meanings of the new words are explained in each lesson, and the ones that you will probably meet again and again are grouped in the ''New words for reading'' section. The exercises after each text will help you not only to understand the ideas in them, but also to discuss them with your classmates and write your own thoughts about them.

We hope you enjoy the book, and would love to hear your ideas about it. Write to us!

About the authors

Caroline Banks lives in Cambridge, Massachusetts. She holds degrees from Smith College, the University of California at Berkeley, and Boston University. She has taught English and Italian on both coasts of the United States, and she has also lived and taught in Italy. She now teaches ESL and Reading at Arlington High School, Arlington, Massachusetts.

Tom Rowe lives in Boston, Massachusetts. He was born and raised in Scotland, and holds degrees from the University of St. Andrews, Scotland; the University of Birmingham, England; and Harvard University. He has lived and taught in the United Kingdom, Belgium, Spain, and Italy, and now lives, teaches, and writes in Boston, Massachusetts.

About the artist

Nicholas Read lives in Cambridge Massachusetts. He holds a degree in painting from the University of North Carolina at Chapel Hill, and degrees in history and law from the University of Virginia. Although a lawyer by necessity, he loves art best.

To the Teacher

Beginning students are often able to recognize much more English in text than they can produce in speech or writing. The purpose of this book is to give students an opportunity to expand that receptive vocabulary while helping them to develop efficient reading skills. In addition, exercises for interaction and writing provide a "bridge" whereby students can make what they have read part of their active vocabulary.

The structure of the book

The lessons are grouped into five sections:
Part One deals with aspects of the planet Earth.
Part Two is a short story in four episodes.
Part Three is a selection of stories, fables, and rhymes.
Part Four deals with disasters, some serious, some not so serious.
Part Five presents stories from Europe, Asia, Africa, and the Americas.

Each lesson begins with prereading exercises. These are designed to help students connect what they already know about a subject with what they are about to read—a kind of bridge between themselves and the text. Skimming and scanning exercises may follow the warm-up activities. These can be done in small groups or as a class.

The text is the main part of each lesson: most of the students' time will be spent in reading it and rereading it. New words are either glossed within the text if they are low-frequency, or presented thematically in the "New words for reading" section if they are high-frequency. Grammar forms are also presented as they appear in the lessons, not so much to be studied, but rather to serve as a reminder of the forms which should be turning up in the students' basal grammar book more or less at the same time.

The activities that follow the text usually begin with a "true or false," cloze, or sequencing exercise designed to foster comprehension of the text and, in most cases, to stimulate a further, more detailed reading. These are followed by activities that focus on the language used in the text, either on the lexis, the structure, or the idiom, and finally by discussion and writing activities that lead beyond the content of the text. Although a lesson may contain any or all of these exercises, we think it is important to remember that the main part of the lesson should be the reading of the text itself and the discussion which leads from it, rather than the "busywork" that can so easily arise from overemphasis on exercises.

What follows is a sample lesson which may illustrate the principles underlying the book. We urge you to try it on your own, or better still, with a colleague.

Demonstration Lesson

Teacher!

Think about it

For twenty-four years Sylvia Ashton-Warner taught five-year-old Maori and white children in a provincial New Zealand school.
1. What do you imagine were some of the problems she faced in the classroom?
2. In teaching reading to a multi-ethnic class, what are some of the issues that the teacher faces?
3. What would you consider to be suitable material for five-year-olds beginning reading?

Organic Reading

Sylvia Ashton-Warner believed that children had to be given texts with which they could become intensely involved. Here is what she says about reading:

> I see the mind of a five-year-old as a volcano with two vents: destructiveness and creativeness. And I see that to the extent that we widen the creative channel, we atrophy the destructive one. And it seems to me that since these words of the key vocabulary are no less than the captions of the dynamic life itself, they course out through the creative channel, making their contribution to the drying up of the destructive vent. From all of which I am constrained to see it as creative reading and to count it among the arts.
>
> First words must mean something to a child.
>
> First words must have intense meaning for a child. They must be part of his being.
>
> How much hangs on the love of reading, the instinctive inclination to hold a book! *Instinctive.* That's what it must be. The reaching out for a book needs to become an organic action, which can happen at this yet formative age. Pleasant words won't do. Respectable words won't do. They must be words organically tied up, organically born from the dynamic life itself. They must be words that are already a part of the child's being. "A child," reads a recent publication on the approach of the American books, "can be led to feel that Janet and John are friends." *Can be led to feel.* Why lead him to feel or try to lead him to feel that these strangers are friends? What about the passionate feeling he has already for his own friends? To me it is inorganic to overlook this step. To me it is an offence against art. I see it as an interruption in the natural expansion of life. . . . (from Sylvia Ashton-Warner, *Teacher.*)

Note: In student lessons side glosses will define all low-frequency words and cultural references. The "New words for reading" section will contain definitions and examples of all high-frequency words.

Exercises

A   True or false

Read these statements, and then read the text again to see whether they are true or false.

1. Sylvia Ashton-Warner claims that the more creative a child is allowed to be, the less destructive he is likely to be.

2. She believes that children at a formative stage will not reach instinctively for a book.

3. She states that the language presented to children in texts should be carefully chosen and graded.

4. She believes that it is wrong to overlook children's passions.

B   Think about it

Sylvia Ashton-Warner uses these phrases:

1. the creative channel

2. the destructive vent

3. Pleasant words won't do. Respectable words won't do.

4. organically born from the dynamic life itself

5. an interruption in the natural expansion of life

What do you understand by each of them? Share ideas with a colleague.

C   Talk about it

1. Do you agree or disagree with Sylvia Ashton-Warner's philosophy of teaching reading? Give your reasons.

2. How do you think reading should be taught?

D   Write about it

Write a paragraph or two agreeing or disagreeing with her philosophy.

This course is founded on the belief that students read best when they are *engaged* in what they are reading. Our purpose has been to present texts which appeal not only to the students' curiousity, but also to their feelings and their imagination. The texts which we have included not only *inform* on subjects from plate tectonics, to the definition of the term "bird," to the spread of the English language—but they also amuse and entertain with stories, songs, rhymes, and fables, and they provoke thought and discussion of "real-life" issues such as fairness and justice, right and wrong, friendship and love, fear and death. These, we believe, are issues which, to paraphrase Sylvia Ashton-Warner, have intense meaning for the adolescent and the young adult.

The exercises are written in a straightforward tone which does not patronize the student. They are designed to foster comprehension of the text, to encourage reflection on the language used, and to stimulate students in relating the subject matter to their own lives. Although the "skills" or "strategies" involved will be obvious to the teacher, we have couched the exercises in clear, nontechnical language which keeps the focus of the lesson on the text and its subject matter.

All texts are authentic and unchanged from the original. Even when extracted from a longer work, they are self-contained and need no introduction other than the one given in the lessons themselves. For the teacher's information, however, we have included historical, geographical, and cultural notes for each lesson in the *Instructor's Manual* accompanying the series, together with an answer key, tests, and notes on the tape program.

We hope you enjoy using *The Day the Mountain Moved* and the other two books in the *Readings in English* series, *Sneakers and Blue Jeans: An Introduction to Fiction* and *One in a Million: People in the News*. We would love to hear from you.

C.B. & T.R.

This book is dedicated to Janie.

PART ONE
THE PLANET EARTH

In this part you will find out some interesting facts and figures about our planet, and about those countries where many people speak English.

WHERE ARE YOU GOING?

SO LONG FOR NOW

A Message to You from Space

Hello Earth Person!

My name is Nick

and I come from Zarko,

a planet of star 123.

I'm studying English.

Our teacher asked us to write you today.

I'm 15,000 years old.

I've been in school since I was 4,000 years old.

I'm learning to drive a Zarko-car.

I love to dance. Tell me about Earth. How many people live
there? Are there animals? Are your plants blue and your
oceans orange? Write soon. Here's my address:

Nick
Box B
Planet Zarko
Star 123
Space

"Where are you calling from?"

What about *you*?

1. Where are you from?
2. What city or town do you live in?
3. What country?
4. What continent?

"Hello! Hello!"

– Hello! Hello! Who's that?
– Where are you?
– Where's that?
– Where's that?
– Where's that?
– Where's that?
– Is it on the planet Earth?

– It's Tom.
– I'm in Edinburgh.
– That's in Scotland.
– In the United Kingdom.
– Europe.
– What? *You don't know?*[1]
– Who are you? And where are you *calling*[2] from?

[1]Don't you know?

– This is Tina. I'm calling from a satellite in space.

Tom is from Edinburgh, Scotland. Edinburgh is a city in Scotland, a part of the United Kingdom. Look at the map. The United Kingdom is part of Europe. Europe is one of the seven continents on the Earth.

5   Where is Tina from? Well, we don't know. She's calling people on the planet Earth from a satellite in space.

New words for reading

Nouns

PLACES:

city (-ies)   a place with many people and many buildings
New York City, Toronto, Edinburgh, and Jackson are cities.
continents(s)   large parts of the earth
There are seven continents on the earth. Count them on the map on page 6.
ocean(s)   large parts of water on the earth
The Atlantic and the Pacific are oceans. Find them on the map on page 6.
satellite(s)   See the picture on page 3.
sea(s)   a small ocean
Find the Caribbean Sea on the map on page 6.
space   See the picture on page 1.

NAMES OF PLACES:

CITIES	COUNTRIES
Canberra	**Australia**
Edinburgh	**Scotland**
Georgetown	**Guyana**
Kingston	**Jamaica**
Manila	**The Philippines**
Nairobi	**Kenya**
New Delhi	**India**
Toronto	**Canada**
Washington, D.C.	**The United States (of America)**
Wellington	**New Zealand**

The United Kingdom (U.K.)   A country in Europe.
England and Scotland are parts of the United Kingdom.

NAMES OF CONTINENTS:	NAMES OF OCEANS:
Africa	**Atlantic Ocean**
Antarctica	**Caribbean Sea**
Asia	**Pacific Ocean**
Australia	
Europe	
North America	
South America	

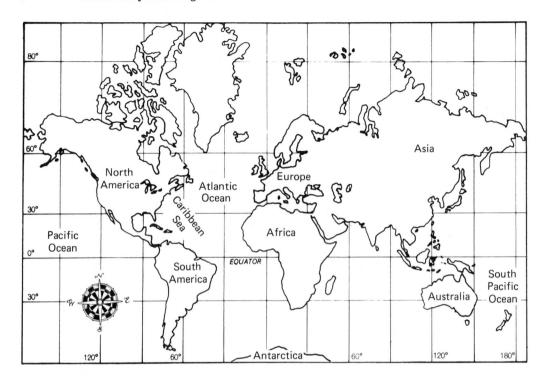

Grammar

Questions and answers

Who's that? It's Tom.
Who are you? This is Tina.
Where are you? I'm in Edinburgh.
Where's that? That's in Scotland.
Where are you calling from? I'm calling from a satellite.

Contractions

A contraction is two words put together with an apostrophe (').
One letter of one of the words is usually dropped.
These contractions are in the Questions and Answers above.

who's = who is
it's = it is
I'm = I am
where's = where is
that's = that is

Exercises

1A Who's that? Where's that?

Read each conversation and answer the questions. Tina is calling from her satellite in space. She's calling all the people in the picture on page 3. Choose from the words in **bold type** (dark letters).

1. – Hello! Who's that?   – It's Sarah.
   – Where are you?   – I'm in Toronto.
   – Where's that?   – In Canada.
   – Where's that?   – In North America.
   – Where's that?   – What? You don't know?

Canada   Toronto   Sarah   North America

a. Who is Tina calling? _____

b. What city is this person from? _____

c. What country is that city in? _____

d. What continent is that country in?_____

2. – Hello! Who's that?   – It's Paul.
   – Where are you?   – I'm in Washington, D.C.
   – Where's that?   – In the United States.
   – Where's that?   – In North America.
   – Where's that?   – What? You don't know?

Paul   North America   Washington, D.C.   The United States

a. Who is Tina calling? _____

b. What city is he from? _____

c. What country is that in? _____

d. What continent is that in? _____

3. – Hello! Who's that?   – It's Anne.
  – Where are you?   – I'm in Canberra.
  – Where's that?   – It's in Australia.
  – Where's that?   – What? You don't know?

Canberra   Australia   Anne

a. Who is Tina calling? _____

b. What city is she from? _____

c. What country and continent is that in? _____

1B Names and places

Put the correct information in the paragraphs. Choose from the names and
places in **bold type**. Use the maps and the reading to help you.

1. Delroy and Marlene   Kingston   Jamaica   Caribbean

_____ ____ _____ are from _____,

_____. _____ is a city in _____.

_____ is a country in the _____.

2. Sanchita   New Delhi   India   Asia

_____ is from ____ _____, _____. ____

_____ is a city in _____. _____ is a country in

_____.

3. Richie   Wellington   New Zealand   South Pacific

_____ is from _____, ____ _____.

_____ is a city in ____ _____.

____ _____ is in the _____ _____.

1C Write about it

Now write paragraphs about other people Tina is calling. Use the paragraphs from 1B to help you.

1. Peter   Nairobi   Kenya   Africa
2. Maria Luisa   Manila   The Philippines   Pacific
3. Winston   Georgetown   Guyana   South America

1D Act it out

Tina is calling *you*! Finish the conversation and perform it with a classmate.

– Hello! Hello! Who's that!   _____

– Where are you?   _____

– Where's that?   _____

– Where's that?   _____

– Where's that?   What! You don't know?

– Is it on the planet Earth?   Tina? Is that you?

– Yes, and I'm calling from the airport.

LESSON

2

Who speaks English?

Think about it

1. What languages do people speak in your country?
2. Name some countries where people speak English.

Ken Karp

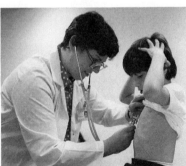

Ken Karp

Liama Druskis

10

United Nations. Photo by Marcia Weistein.

British Information Services

Irene Springer

Liama Druskis

Shirley Zeiberg

Liama Druskis

11

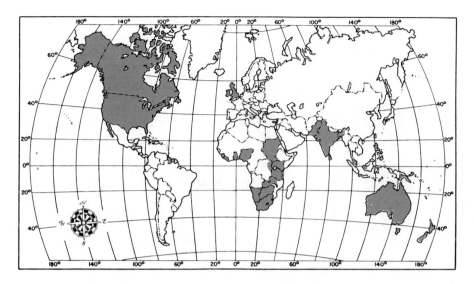

Not only the English speak English!

Of course the English speak English: they gave the language its name. English is spoken also in other parts of Great Britain—in Scotland and Wales, and in Ireland, too. And it is spoken on other continents. *In fact*[1] English is now
5   the language of many hundreds of millions of people all over the world.

When Europeans colonized other lands, they spread their languages to all parts of the world. *Nearly*[2] all of those lands are independent countries now, not colonies, but many of
10 the people still speak the languages of the colonizers. English is spoken today in many of the lands colonized by the British, *such as*[3] Australia, Canada, Guyana, New Zealand, the United States, and many of the islands in the Caribbean.
15 In some countries many different languages are spoken. Sometimes this is a *problem:*[4] how can people with different native languages understand each other? One *solution*[5] is to use English: people speak their own language in their own part of the country, or at home, but they use English to
20 communicate with people who live in parts of their country where other languages are spoken. This is how English is used in countries such as India, the Philippines, and in many parts of Africa and the Pacific.

[1] the truth is
[2] almost
[3] like; for example
[4] difficulty
[5] answer

²⁵ English is now the language of many of the world's people. There are different ways of speaking and pronouncing English in different parts of the world, but we can usually understand each other.

New words for reading

Nouns

colonizer(s)   people who colonize
Colonizers came to North and South America from Europe many years ago.

colony(ies)   a land far from a "parent" country
People from England went to North America to start colonies in the 1600s.

land(s)   countries, places
People use English in many different lands.

language(s)   what people talk, understand, read and write
People use many different languages.

world(s)   earth
Look at the map of the world. Can you find your country?

MORE NAMES OF PLACES:

Great Britain
Wales
Ireland

NOUNS OF NATIONALITY:

the British *(plural)*   the people from Great Britain
the English *(plural)*   the people from England
European(s)   person(s) from Europe

Adjectives

independent   standing alone; not part of another country
Most countries that were colonies are now independent.

major   most important, most used
What is the major language in your country?

native   born, coming from
What is Dan's native land? He was born in Ireland.

Verbs

to colonize (colonized)   to stay and live in a colony
  The British colonized parts of North America, Africa, and Asia.

to communicate (communicated)   to make others know or understand
  We can communicate now: we both speak the same language.

to pronounce (pronounced)   to say the sounds of a language

Idioms and expressions

each other   I understand *you*. You understand *me*. We understand **each other**.

Grammar

Words in the same "family"

Look at the way the word "colony" changes. The end of the word changes, but not the main part: **colon-**.

Verbs: **to colonize**
Noun: **colony, colonies** (*place*)
Noun: **colonizer, colonizers** (*person*)

The Passive Voice, Present Tense

to speak:

English **is spoken**. = People speak English.
Other languages **are spoken** also. = People speak other languages, too.

to use:

English **is used** to communicate. = People use English to communicate.

Irregular Simple Past forms

to give   The English **gave** the language its name.
to spread   The Europeans **spread** their languages to all parts of the world.

Exercises

2A New words

Fill in the blanks. Choose from the words in **bold type**.

languages   world   spoken   native   communicate   colonized

English is spoken all over the _____. It is _____

in Great Britain and in Ireland, and also in the lands which were

_____ by the British. In some countries where many

_____ are spoken, English is used so that people who have

different _____ languages can _____ with each

other.

2B True or false

Read these statements and then read the text again to find out whether they are true or false.

_____ 1. English is now the language of more than a hundred million people all over the world.
_____ 2. All the lands which used to be British colonies are now independent countries.
_____ 3. There are not many different ways of speaking and pronouncing English.

2C Countries and languages

Some countries have one major language. For example, French is the major language of France. Here are some countries with a major language. Match the language with the country.

_____ **1.** Chinese   **a.** Denmark
_____ **2.** Danish   **b. France**
__b__ **3. French**   **c.** Sweden
_____ **4.** Italian   **d.** Poland
_____ **5.** Japanese   **e.** Italy
_____ **6.** Korean   **f.** Korea
_____ **7.** Polish   **g.** Thailand
_____ **8.** Portuguese   **h.** China
_____ **9.** Swedish   **i.** Japan
_____ **10.** Thai   **j.** Portugal

3

Continents on the Move

Look and answer

1. Find your country on Map A.
2. Can you find it on Map B?

The World: Past, Present, and Future

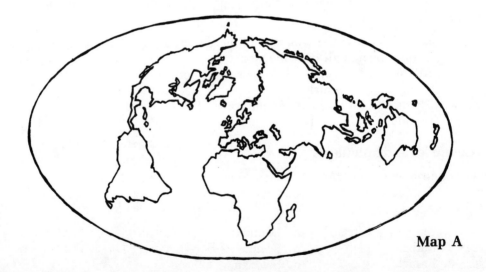

Map A

This map of the world looks familiar to us. But many *geologists*[1] believe that the earth looked very different fifty *million*[2] years ago. They believe that the continents were all joined in one big "supercontinent," *perhaps*[3] like the one in
5 Map B:

[1] people who study geology, the science of the earth
[2] 1 million = 1,000,000
[3] maybe

16

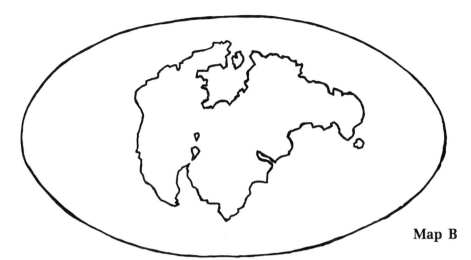

Map B

Gradually[4] the "supercontinent" divided into huge pieces that moved away in different *directions.*[5] Over millions and millions of years, *the Americas*[6] moved west, Australia moved east, Antarctica moved south, Europe and [10] Africa moved north, and India moved up against Asia, *forming*[7] the great mountains which we know as the Himalayas.

Geologists believe that our continents are still moving. They say this is why we have earthquakes, the short, fast [15] movements at the earth's *surface.*[8] As the continents move, they shake. If the continents are moving, perhaps in another fifty million years our planet will look very different.

[4] slowly, over a long time

5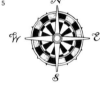

[6] North and South America and the Caribbean islands

[7] making

[8] top

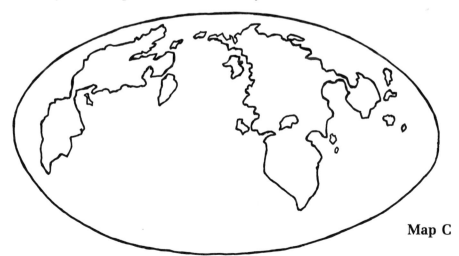

Map C

Can you find your country on *this* strange map?

New words for reading

Nouns

earthquake(s)   shaking and moving of the earth
movement(s)   when something moves
supercontinent(s)   very large continent

Adjectives

OPPOSITES:

familiar   something we know; the same
  Map A looks familiar.
strange   something we don't know; different
  Maps B and C look strange.

Numbers

one hundred   100
one thousand   1,000
one million   1,000,000
fifty million 50,000,000

Verbs

to believe   to think that something is true
  Many geologists believe the earth looked different fifty million years ago.
to divide   to break into pieces; to separate
  The supercontinent divided into huge pieces.
to join   to put together; opposite of to divide
  The continents were all joined.
to move   to go to a different place
  The continents are moving.
to shake   to make short, fast movements
  As the continents move, they shake.

Idioms and expressions

on the move   moving

Grammar

Cause and effect

Why do things happen?
Read these sentences. What happens? Why does it happen?

1. **The continents move.** *(cause)*
   Then what happens?
2. **The earth shakes.** *(effect)*
   Then what happens?
3. **We have earthquakes.** *(effect)*
4. **Why** do we have earthquakes?
   Because the continents are still moving.
5. We have earthquakes **because** the continents are still moving.

Exercises

3A True or false

Read these statements and then read the text again to find out whether they are true or false.

_____ 1. All geologists believe that the continents are moving.
_____ 2. It took many millions of years for the "supercontinent" to divide into smaller continents.
_____ 3. The Himalayas are continents.
_____ 4. Earthquakes happen because the continents are still moving.

3B New words

Fill in the blanks. Choose from the words in **bold type.**

different	**directions**	**earthquakes**	**million**
moving	**map**	**moved**	**believe**

The _____ of the world looks very familiar to us, but fifty

_____ years ago it looked very _____.

Geologists _____ that a "supercontinent" divided, and the

pieces _____ away in different _____; this

movement of the earth causes _____. It is strange to think that

our continents are still _____.

3C Think about it

Many geologists believe that our continents are moving, but some do not. What do you think? Is it possible for continents to move?

The Planet Earth

Guess!

1. How many pounds or kilograms does your chair weigh?
2. How much do you weigh?
3. How much do you guess a bus weighs?
4. How much does the water in the Atlantic Ocean weigh?
5. How much does the earth weigh?

Big Ideas

The earth weighs six and a half quintillion tons.

The area of the earth measures almost 200 million square miles. Almost 71 percent of this area is water. The land area is 29 percent.

New words for reading

Nouns

area   an amount of surface; space on the top

How much of the area of the earth is water?

measurement(s)   numbers that tell how long, how wide, how high things are

percentage(s)   numbers that tell the parts of one hundred

percent
0% = none
1% = almost none
99% = almost all
100% = all

weight(s)   numbers that tell how much something weighs

Pounds, tons, and kilograms are used to measure weight.

Measurements of weight and area

1 pound (lb.) = almost ½ kilogram (.453 kilograms)

1 ton = 2,000 pounds = almost 1,000 kilograms (909 kilos)

1 mile = 1.6 kilometers

1 square mile =

Verbs

to guess to predict; to suppose without enough information.
I guess the chair weighs 15 pounds.

to measure

1. to have or be a certain size

   The area of the earth measures 200 million square miles.

2. to find out the size of something

   Please measure the sugar before you put it in the coffee.

to weigh

1. to have or be a certain weight

   The earth weighs a lot!

2. to find out how much something weighs

   Please weigh this fish for me.

Big numbers

one billion   1,000,000,000

one trillion	1,000,000,000,000
one quadrillion	1,000,000,000,000,000
one quintillion	1,000,000,000,000,000,000
one sextillion	1,000,000,000,000,000,000,000

Grammar

Questions and answers

How much?

How much of the area of the earth is water? 71%

How much do you weigh? I weigh...pounds (kilos).

How much does that book weigh? It weighs almost five pounds (more than two kilos).

How many?

How many pounds are in one kilogram? 2.2.

How many zeros in one trillion? One quadrillion?

Exercises

4A Big numbers in English

The earth weighs six and a half quintillion tons. Write this as a number:

_____

4B A word problem

How many pounds does the earth weigh? (Remember: 1 ton = 2,000 pounds.)

4C The area of the earth

Choose the best answer.
1. The area of the earth is more than 71%
    _____.
    a. land
    b. water
    c. area
2. 71% is _____ 29%.
    a. as much as
    b. much more than
    c. much less than
3. The area of the earth is almost 200 million square miles.
    _____ of this area is land.
    a. Almost 142 million square miles
    b. Almost 200 million square miles
    c. Almost 52 million square miles

In this part you will meet people from different parts of the English-speaking world—from Australia, from the United Kingdom, and from the United States—at a summer camp in Canada.

!niaga raor o aragaiN

PART TWO
NIAGARA, O ROAR AGAIN!

Talk about it

What do you think of when you see these words? Tell the class.

airplane	camp	roar	postcards
trip	map	friends	New York
summer	waterfall	Canada	

Dear Aunt Lily,
We're having a wonderful time. Do you
see the strange words
on the other side of
this card? Try read-
ing them backwards!
Love, Arlette

NIAGARA FALLS, NEW YORK

The American Falls as seen from the Gorge Obser-
vation Tower.

Miss Lily Johnson
43 Front Street
Middletown, Ohio
U.S.A.

Buffalo Bill Cody USA 15

Off to Camp in Canada

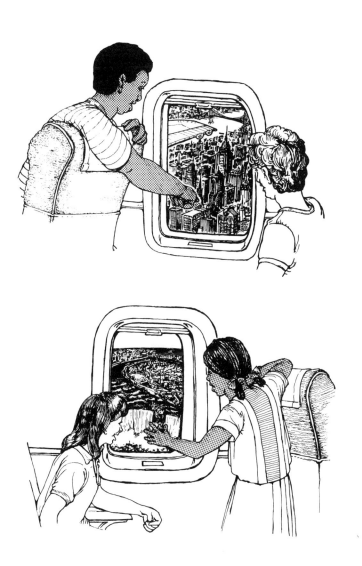

Look and answer

Look at the people in the pictures.

1. Where are they?
2. What are they looking at?

Look at the map

1. Find New York City. What country is it in?
2. Find Toronto. What country is it in?
3. Find Niagara Falls. What countries are they in?

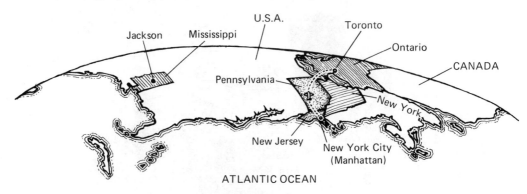

Flight 509

Think about it

1. Do you live in a big city, a small city, or a town?
2. How many people live there?

Flight 509

Charles, Arlette, Kaye, and Tim are on Flight 509 from New York City to Toronto. They're going to Canada, to summer camp, where they will stay for three weeks.

"Look!" says Charles. "That's Manhattan, the center of
5 New York City! Look at that! There's a lot of *traffic*[1] down there!"

"*Incredible!*"[2] says Tim excitedly. "Look at all those *skyscrapers!*[3] Are there any skyscrapers *like*[4] those in your city?"

[1] cars and trucks crowding the roads
[2] I can't believe it.
[3] very tall buildings
[4] similar to

10   "Not like these," says Charles. "I'm from Jackson, Mississippi. It's small, much smaller than New York. Jackson has about two hundred thousand people. New York has a *lot* more than that. What about you? Where are you from?"

15   "I'm from England," says Tim, "from a really small village. Andermere. There are only three hundred and fifty people in it, so everybody knows everybody else."

"And there are no skyscrapers, right?" says Charles with a laugh.

20   "No, no skyscrapers!" laughs Tim.

The plane flies over the green countryside of the states of New Jersey, Pennsylvania, and New York. The weather is so clear that every mountain, every river, and every lake *can be seen.*[5]

25   A flight attendant comes by with drinks.

"Something to drink?" the attendant asks. "Lemonade, orange juice, apple juice, tomato juice, soda?"

"Orange soda, please," says Tim.

"The same for me, please," says Charles.

30   "I'll have some orange juice, please," says Arlette.

"Lemonade for me, thanks," says Kaye.

Soon the captain's *voice*[6] *is heard.*[7] At first he doesn't speak very clearly, so it is difficult to understand what he is saying.

35   "Ladies and gentlemen, we are now flying over the border between the United States and Canada. Look out of the windows on the right, and you will see the great Niagara Falls."

"Oh, Arlette, look!" Kaye cries. "Niagara Falls! I have a
40   *poster*[8] of Niagara in my bedroom at home in Australia! I'm so excited! I can't believe it! I'm really here!"

"That really is something," says Arlette. "Isn't it great?"

The captain's voice is heard again:

"Ladies and gentlemen, in a few minutes we'll be
45   *landing*[9] at the international airport in Toronto. *On behalf of*[10] the crew, thank you for flying with us this afternoon. We hope your flight was *pleasant,*[11] and that you will *enjoy*[12] your stay in Canada."

"Enjoy it?!" cries Kaye, shaking Arlette's arm. "Enjoy
50   it?! I'm going to *love* it!"

[5] they can see
[6] sound of speaking
[7] they hear
[8] large picture
[9] coming down
[10] for
[11] good; nice
[12] like

New words for reading

Nouns

PLACES:

border(s)
country(-ies)
countryside
island(s)
lake(s)
mountain(s)
river(s)
state(s)

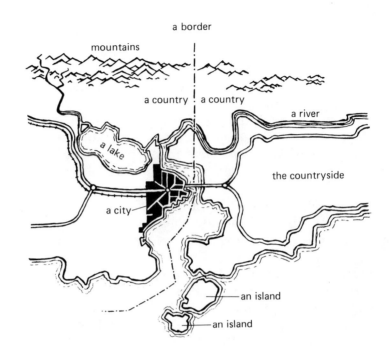

NAMES OF PLACES: (Look at the map on page 132)

SOME COUNTRIES

Australia
Canada
England
The United States of America (The U.S.A.)

SOME STATES OF THE U.S.A. (Look at the map on page 133)

Mississippi
New Jersey
New York
Pennsylvania

SOME CITIES AND TOWNS

Jackson, Mississippi, U.S.A.
Manhattan (part of **New York City**), **New York, U.S.A.**
Niagara Falls, U.S.A. and **Niagara Falls, Canada** (on the border)
Toronto, Ontario, Canada

Persons:

captain(s)   pilot of an airplane

flight attendant(s)   person who helps passengers on an airplane

crew   people who work on an airplane or ship

Things:

camp(s)/summer camp   A place where a group of people go, to stay for a few weeks or months, often on vacation.

Summer camps for young people are usually away from the city.

Things to drink:

juice(s)   apple juice, orange juice, tomato juice

Apple juice is a drink made from apples.

lemonade   the juice of lemons with sugar

soda(s)

Adjectives and adverbs

Some adjectives + **-ly** are adverbs.

Adjectives

excited: I'm so **excited!**

clear: The weather is **clear.**

The captain's voice isn't **clear**.

Adverbs

excitedly: Kaye shouts **excitedly.**

clearly: I can see very **clearly.**

He doesn't speak **clearly**.

Nouns and verbs

Some verb forms are the same, or almost the same as the noun.

to laugh:

''Don't **laugh** at me!'' Tim says with a **laugh**.

to stay:

How long **are** you **staying** in Canada? Our **stay** will be three weeks.

to fly:

We're **flying** to Toronto on **Flight** 509.

Words that have more than one meaning:

so

1. that is why

   There are only 350 people in my village, so (that is why) everybody knows everybody else.

2. very

   I'm so (very) excited!

3. so...that

   The weather is so clear that you can see every mountain. (You can see every mountain because the weather is very clear.)

really

1. it's true; truly

   I'm really (truly) here.

2. very

   I'm from a really (very) small village.

Idioms and expressions

That **really is something.**   That really is big, important, or incredible.

Off to camp!   Going to camp. Starting the trip to camp.

What about you?   Tell me about you.

Grammar

Verbs that tell the future

going to + verb: I'm **going to love** it!

will + verb: They **will stay** in Canada for three weeks.

   I'll have some orange juice. (I'll = I will)
   Look out the window and you **will see** Niagara Falls.

Describing two things

small/smaller than:
Jackson is **small**. What about Andermere? It's **smaller**.
Andermere is **smaller than** Jackson.

Jackson, Mississippi is a **small** city. New York City is not!
Jackson is much **smaller than** New York City.

more than:
Andermere has 350 people. Jackson has 200,000.
Jackson has **more than** Andermere.

Jackson has 200,000 people. New York City has a lot **more**.
New York City has a lot **more than** Jackson.

Exercises

5A True or false

Read these statements and then read the text again to find out
whether they are true or false.
_____ **1.** Charles can see cars from the window of the plane.
_____ **2.** Charles is from Jackson, Mississippi.
_____ **3.** Tim knows everybody in his village.
_____ **4.** Kaye knows about Niagara Falls.
_____ **5.** Arlette has a poster of Niagara Falls.

5B New words

Fill in the blanks. Choose from the words in **bold type**. (You may use a word
more than once.)

New Jersey	**every**	**from**	**countryside**	**Niagara Falls**	**to**
Pennsylvania	**clear**	**center**	**New York**	**border**	

The flight _____ New York _____ Toronto is very pleasant. If

the weather is _____ you can see everything, every mountain,

_____ river, _____ lake. First, you fly over Manhattan, the

_____ of New York City. Then you fly out over the green _____ of

the states of _____, _____, and _____. Soon you cross the

_____ between the United States and Canada, where you have a

wonderful view of the great _____ _____.

5C Act it out

Imagine you are on Flight 509. With your classmates, take the parts of Tim,
Charles, Arlette, Kaye, the flight attendant, and the captain.

5D Write about it

Canada's only border is with the United States. The United States has two
borders, one with Canada and one with Mexico. Great Britain is an island.
   List the countries that have borders with your country. If your country is an
island, list its neighbors.

Niagara, here we come!

Read and decide

These are the postcards that the four friends sent home.
Read these questions. Then read the postcards and find the
answers.

1. Who is Charles's roommate?
2. Who is Arlette's twin?
3. Who lives on a sheep farm?
4. Where are the friends going tomorrow?

Postcards Home

Porterfield/Chickering, Photo Researchers

Dear Mum and Dad,
Camp is terrific! This is a picture of
Toronto. We had a good flight there
yesterday. I am making a lot of
friends. Charles is my roommate. He
is from the USA. His twin sister, Arlette, is in camp, too. She is very
quiet, but nice. We are going to
see Niagara Falls tomorrow.
Love, Tim

Mr. and Mrs. G. Lindsay
12 Bank Street
Andermere
Cumbria CA9 6LT

ENGLAND

TORONTO, ONTARIO, CANADA. A magnificent
aerial view of the city looking toward Lake
Ontario

TORONTO. ONTARIO. CANADA. Magnifique
vue aérienne de la ville qui montre le Lac Onta
rio

Toronto

Dear Mom and Daddy and James
and Libby,
Canada is a nice place. I like
camp a lot. My roommate,
Kaye is from Australia. Her
mom has a sheep farm. Her
daddy died when she was
very little. We're going to
visit Niagara Falls tomorrow.
Lots and lots and lots
of love, Arlette
Hi love from me too!
Charles

The Edwards Family
1163 Roosevelt Drive
Jackson MS 34201
U. S. A.

SUNRISE OVER TORONTO SKYLINE
LEVER DU SOLEIL AU-DESSUS DU PROFIL DE L'HORIZON DE
TORONTO

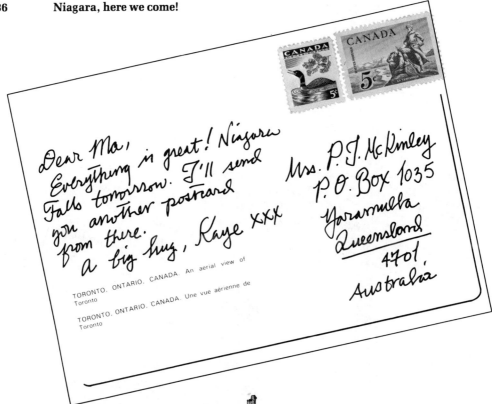

Dear Ma,
Everything is great! Niagara
Falls tomorrow. I'll send
you another postcard
from there.
a big hug, Kaye xxx

Mrs. P. J. McKinley
P. O. Box 1035
Yarranulla
Queensland
4701,
Australia

TORONTO, ONTARIO, CANADA. An aerial view of
Toronto

TORONTO, ONTARIO, CANADA. Une vue aérienne de
Toronto

Big? Huge? Enormous!

Imagine fifteen buses standing
one on top of the other.

The next morning at nine o'clock *sharp*[1] a big yellow bus left the camp for Niagara Falls. Everyone inside the bus was very excited.

"Come on, Kaye," said Arlette excitedly. "Tell us about
⁵ Niagara Falls."

"You visited them when you were little, right?" asked Charles.

"No, but my Ma came to see them with my Dad," said Kaye. "That was before I was born. They were on their
¹⁰ honeymoon. A lot of people go to Niagara on their honeymoons."

"That's romantic," said Arlette, dreamily.[2]

"So,[3] tell us about Niagara," said Tim, *impatiently*.[4]

"Well," began Kaye, "my Ma says that the falls are really
¹⁵ big. I mean huge...I mean enormous...I mean..."

"How big?" asked Charles.

"The guide book says they are 56 meters high and 328 meters wide at their highest and widest," said Kaye.

"That's...about 180 feet high and...over 1,000 feet wide,"
²⁰ said Tim, scratching his head. Tim was very good at mathematics.

"Wow!" said Charles. "That's fifteen times as high as this bus! Imagine fifteen buses like this one, standing one on top of the other. Imagine! Fifteen! Wow!"

²⁵ "And you have to wear a raincoat and a hat," continued Kaye, "because even when it's *not* raining, it *seems to be raining*![5] There's so much water in the air."

"Incredible!" said Tim.

"And the water makes so much noise that you can hear it
³⁰ for miles and miles around," said Kaye. "It makes so much noise that..."

"Listen!" shouted Arlette. "Listen, everybody!"

The bus stopped in the parking lot. *In the distance*[6] they saw the white *mist*[7] of Niagara Falls, and through the wet
³⁵ air they heard the roar of Niagara's water, like a thousand angry lions in a *cage*.[8]

"We're here!" shouted Kaye. "We're here!"

[1] exactly
[2] as if dreaming
[3] well; now
[4] not wanting to wait
[5] looks like it's raining
[6] far away
[7] water in the air like a cloud
[8]

New words for reading

Nouns

guide book(s)   book that gives information about a place
  A guide book often has maps.

honeymoon(s)   vacation after getting married

  My parents went to Florida on their honeymoon.

hug(s)

roar(s)   noise like a lion's voice: r-r-r-R-R-R!!

roommate(s)   person who shares a room with another

sheep   (singular and plural)

twin   one of two persons born together to the same mother

NOUNS THAT TELL "HOW LONG":

foot (feet)   1 foot = 0.305 meters

meter(s)   1 meter = 3.28 feet

mile(s)   1 mile = 5,280 feet or 1,609.34 meters

miles and miles   many miles

You can hear the roar of Niagara for miles and miles.

NOUNS THAT MEAN THE SAME:

Mother: Mum (U.K.); **mom** (U.S.A.); **Ma** (Australia and U.S.A.)

Father: Dad; Daddy

Adjectives

romantic   giving the feeling of love

The moon over Niagara is so romantic!

wet   with water; not dry; rainy

My shoes are wet. The weather is wet.

DESCRIBING SIZE (HOW BIG):

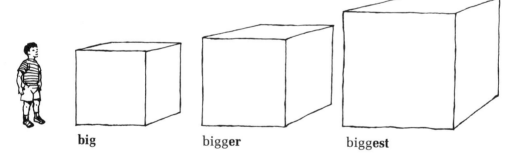

big   bigger   bigg**est**

wide   wid**er**   wid**est**

high   higher   highest

OTHER ADJECTIVES THAT MEAN VERY BIG:

huge   *New York City is huge.*
enormous   *Niagara Falls is enormous.*

Verb

to imagine   to think about
Imagine 15 buses, one on top of the other!
Imagine you are at Niagara Falls.

Idioms and expressions

Here we come!   We're coming now.
one on top of the other   one thing standing on the other
Wow!   Says you are excited.

Grammar

Using verbs with ''-ing'' to describe:

scratching (to scratch)

''That's over 1000 feet wide,'' said Tim, **scratching** his head.

standing (to stand = to be)

Fifteen buses **standing** one on top of the other.

Comparing two things. Look at the picture on page 36.

as...as:

One Niagara Falls = 15 buses.
Niagara Falls is 15 times **as** high **as** one bus.

Verbs in the Simple Past Tense

Look at these sentences with **to be** in the Simple Past Tense.
They describe the past (yesterday and before).

1. Where **are** you now? Where **were** you yesterday?
2. We**'re** at camp today. We **were** at Niagara Falls yesterday.
3. I **am** tired today. I **was** so excited yesterday.

Irregular Simple Past forms of verbs

to come	My Ma **came** to see Niagara Falls with my Dad.
to die	Her daddy **died** when she was little.
to have	We **had** a good flight yesterday.
to hear	They **heard** the roar of Niagara's water.
to leave	The bus **left** at nine sharp.

to see	They **saw** the white mist of Niagara Falls.
to send	These are the postcards they **sent** home.
to stop	The bus **stopped** in the parking area.

Simple Past forms of verbs that describe talking

to ask	**asked**
to begin	**began**
to continue	**continued**
to say	**said**
to shout	**shouted**

Exercises

6A True or false

Read these statements and then read the text again to find out whether they are true or false.

_____ **1.** Kaye came to Niagara Falls with her mother and father.
_____ **2.** Niagara Falls is as high as fifteen buses, one on top of the other.
_____ **3.** It is always raining at Niagara Falls.
_____ **4.** The water makes a lot of noise.

6B New words

Complete the story. Choose from the verbs in **bold type**. Remember to put each verb in the Simple Past tense.

arrive   be   go   have   hear   leave   see   stop   visit

Arlette, Charles, Kaye, and Tim _____ a good flight from New

York to Toronto, although when they _____ at camp, they

_____ a little tired. The next day, they _____ Niagara

Falls. The bus _____ camp at nine o'clock. When the bus

_____ in the parking lot, they _____ the roar of

Niagara's water. When they _____ closer, they _____ the

white mist of the falls.

6C Talk about it

Niagara Falls is a very popular place for a honeymoon. Kaye's Mom and Dad went there all the way from Australia.

1. Do people in your country go on honeymoons?
2. Which places in your country do people think are romantic? Why?

7

r-r-r-R-R-R-Roar!

Look and answer

Look at the picture. The water going over Niagara Falls makes a *lot* of noise.

1. What is the loudest noise you can remember?
2. What is the loudest noise you can imagine?
3. Tell your classmates about it.

Maid of the Mist

"You look so funny!" shouted Arlette above the noise of the water.

"*I* look funny? What about *you*?!" shouted Tim.

Everybody was wearing blue raincoats with hoods that
⁵ were much too big. And everybody looked very funny indeed.

The *Maid of the Mist* sailed towards the falls. Water came *crashing*[1] down like a terrible rainstorm: millions and

[1] falling, making a loud noise

millions of tons of water that now sounded like millions
10 and millions of angry lions.

Kaye looked up at the falls: white water, white water, and
more white water. Arlette took off her hood and laughed as
the spray wet her hair. Charles and Tim were laughing, too.
They were trying to speak to each other, but they could not
15 hear: the water was too loud.

"Let's all scream our hardest!" shouted Charles.

"What did you say?" shouted Tim. "I can't hear a
word!"

Charles pointed to his mouth. "Read my *lips*,"[2] he said,
20 slowly. "When I count to three, let's all scream. Okay?"

Kaye and Arlette nodded their heads.

Charles waved his hand and counted: one...two...
THREE! And four heads went back, four mouths opened
wide, and four voices screamed and screamed and
25 screamed.

"Aaaaaaaaaaaaaaah!"

But the only thing that anybody could hear was the roar
of the white water of Niagara.

[3] able to be seen,
then unable to be
seen

The *Maid of the Mist* sailed closer to the roaring falls.
30 "Tim!" Kaye shouted. "How high are the falls? I forget."
Nobody answered.

"Where's Tim?" asked Kaye.

"He's...." Charles looked around. "He's not here."

"Look!" cried Arlette, pointing at the angry white water
35 below. "Look! Oh, no!!"

A blue raincoat was *appearing and disappearing*[3] in the
bubbling foam.[4] The three friends looked at each other.

"Let's find Tim," said Kaye calmly. But she wasn't calm.

New words for reading

Nouns

hood(s)

storm(s)   when a lot of rain or snow falls and the wind blows

Adjectives

How big?

big   **too big**   **much too big**

How funny?

funny   **so funny**   **very funny indeed**

Verbs

A verb form can sometimes be the same as the adjective form:

Adjective: Arlette's hair was very **wet**.

Verb: She laughed as the spray **wet** her hair.

The verb ''to look'' can have more than one meaning:

to look at/to look + adjective/**to look up at:**
Look at Arlette!
She **looks funny** in that hat.
Kaye's **looking up at** the falls.

Verbs with ''like:''

to be like   to be the same
to look like   to look the same
to sound like   to sound the same; to make the same noise

More regular (-ed) **Simple Past forms:**

to count   to name numbers
Charles **counted** to three: one, two, three.

to laugh   Arlette took off her hat and **laughed**.

to look at   to move your eyes toward
Everybody **looked at** the funny hats.

to nod   to move your head up and down; to say ''yes'' with your head
Kaye and Arlette **nodded** their heads.

to open
Four mouths **opened** wide.

to point to
Charles **pointed to** his mouth.

to sail   to move across the water
The *Maid of the Mist* **sailed** towards the falls.

to scream   to shout very loudly
Four voices **screamed** and **screamed**.
to sound like   to make the same noise
The water **sounded like** angry lions.
to wave   to move your hand and arm from side to side
Charles **waved** his hand and counted.

Idioms and expressions

Let's scream our hardest.   Let's scream very, very loud.

Grammar

Questions in the Simple Past with "did"

Present: What **do** you **say**? What **does** she **say**?
Past: What **did** you **say**? What **did** she **say**?

Past Progressive Tense

Compare the Present Progressive with the Past Progressive.
Present Progressive:

1. Everybody **is wearing** raincoats.
2. Charles and Tim **are laughing**.
3. They **are trying** to speak.

Past Progressive:

1. Everybody **was wearing** raincoats.
2. Charles and Tim **were laughing**.
3. They **were trying** to speak.

can/could

Compare the Present with the Past.
Present: I **can** see but I **can't** hear now.
Past: I **could** see but I **couldn't** hear before.

Exercises

7A True or false

_____ 1.   They could not hear each other because of the noise of the boat.
_____ 2.   Kaye and Arlette took off their hoods.
_____ 3.   Kaye wanted to ask Tim a question about the falls.
_____ 4.   The friends saw a raincoat down in the water.

7B Who said what?

Decide whether it was Kaye, Tim, Arlette, or Charles who said the following.

1. ''Tim and I were trying to talk, but we couldn't hear a word. The noise of

    the water was much too loud.'' _____

2. ''I took off my hood, and the spray wet my hair. It was great!'' _____

3. ''Arlette said I looked funny in my raincoat and hood. She looked funny,

    too!'' _____

4. ''The boys were screaming their loudest, so Arlette and I screamed, too.''

    _____

7C Talk about it

The kids on the boat screamed and screamed. Do you think that was a funny
thing to do? Why or why not?

LESSON

Guess who!

Think about it

1. Do you know the man in the photo?
2. What do you know about him?

AFL-CIO News

Talk about it

1. Get together with classmates and find out what they know about Martin Luther King, Jr.
2. Make a list of questions about him.

Where *were* you?

"Tim!" cried Arlette when they got off the boat after the trip into the falls. "Where *were* you, for heaven's sake? We looked for you everywhere."

"I was over there," said Tim. "I was..."

5   "We were *worried*[1] about you," said Kaye. "Where's your raincoat?"

"I lost it," began Tim. "I..."

"We thought you'd fallen in," said Charles. "We thought we saw your coat in the water."

10   "That *was* my raincoat," said Tim. "I..."

"*You gave us a scare*,"[2] said Kaye. "Where did you go?"

"I went over to the..." began Tim.

"You didn't tell us where you were going," said Arlette. "We were worried. We thought you..."

15   "Hey! Hey! Hey!" Tim shouted. "Will you please listen to me?"

They looked at him, surprised.

[1] frightened
[2] you scared us

"Thank you," he said, laughing. "First, it *was* my coat you saw in the water. It was too big, and it looked funny, so I took it off. Then it fell in the water. Second, I went to tell the *camp counselor*[3] about it: he's standing over there. And third, I *did* tell you I was going, but you didn't hear me because you were shouting like crazy."

"Oh," said Arlette.

"Well," said Kaye.

"I don't think you'll get that raincoat back now." said Charles. "I'm sure glad you weren't wearing it when it fell in."

"Me, too!" said Tim.

Twenty Questions

What a day! Back at camp, tired, but very *pleased*[4] with their visit to the *spectacular*[5] Niagara Falls, everyone *took a rest*[6] before dinner. Tim wrote all about Niagara in his *diary.*[7] Kaye sent a postcard to her mother with a picture of the *Maid of the Mist.* Arlette *brushed*[8] her lovely black hair which was still wet with Niagara's water. And Charles, who was completely *exhausted,*[9] lay down for a short *nap.*[10]

After dinner, however, everybody was *full of energy*[11] again. Sitting around the *campfire,*[12] they told stories, sang songs, toasted *marshmallows on sticks over the flames.*[13]

"Let's play a game," said Tim.

"Okay. What'll we play?" asked Kaye.

"I know," said Charles. "I'm thinking of a person. Guess who it is."

"Is the person female?" asked Tim.

"No," said Charles.

"Male," said Arlette.

"Of course!" said Charles.

[3] person who is like a teacher at camp
[4] happy
[5] great, wonderful to see
[6] took time to not move or work
[7] book you use for writing down what happens each day
[8]
[9] very, very tired
[10] few minutes' sleep
[11] moving; feeling strong
[12] See picture.
[13] See picture. Marshmallows are soft, white candies.

"Is he alive?" asked Kaye.   [14] answered

20   "No, he's dead," said Charles.

"Is he American?" asked Tim.

"Yes," said Charles.

"Is it Martin Luther King, Jr.?" asked Arlette.

"Yes! How did you guess?" asked Charles.

25   "Because you *always* choose Martin Luther King, Jr. when
we play this game!" laughed Arlette.

"Okay! Okay! I have one!" shouted Kaye. "I'm thinking
of a person. Guess who it is."

"Is the person male?" asked Charles.

30   "No, female," said Kaye.

"Is she alive?" asked Arlette.

"Yes," *replied*[14] Kaye.

"Is she American?" asked Tim.

"No."

35   "Is she British?" asked Charles.

"No."

"Is she Australian?" asked Arlette.

"Yes," said Kaye with a smile.

"IT'S YOU!!" shouted everybody together.

40   "Of course!" laughed Kaye.

New words for reading

Nouns

nationality (-ies)   the nation or country a person or thing comes from
   What's your nationality?

occupation(s)   the job a person does
   What's his occupation?

female (f.)   woman or girl; she

male (m.)   man or boy; he

Adjectives

alive   living now; not dead
   You are alive.

dead   not living now; not alive
   Martin Luther King, Jr. is dead.

SOME ADJECTIVES OF NATIONALITY:
American   from North or South America

Australian	from Australia
Canadian	from Canada
British	from Britain

Idioms and expressions

Guess who?   Guess who it is. Think and try to imagine who it is.

Of course!   Yes!

For heaven's sake!   Really!

What a day!   This is a wonderful, exciting day.

Like crazy!   Like a crazy person. Very loud.

Grammar

Making questions in the Simple Past

Did you **see** that? Yes, I **did**.

What **did** you **ask**? We **asked** a question.

What **did** he **play**? He **played** Twenty Questions.

What **did** they **sing**? They **sang** songs.

When **did** the game **begin**? It **began** an hour ago.

Irregular (not -ed) Past forms

to fall in	It was Tim's coat that **fell in** the water.
	We were afraid Tim **had fallen in** the water.
to lie down	Charles **lay down** for a short nap.
to lose	I **lost** my raincoat.
to take	**Everyone took** a short rest before dinner.
to tell	They **told** stories.
to sing	They **sang** songs.
to write	Tim **wrote** all about Niagara.

Exercises

8A Play Twenty Questions

Think of a person. Your classmates ask questions. Answer only "Yes" or "No." If they can't guess correctly after 20 questions, you win. (Read the text again if you can't remember how to play.)

8B Play another game

Do you know any more guessing games? Think of the best one you know. Explain it to the class and show how to play it.

Something funny, something sad.
Life's never *all* good.
It's *never* all bad.
Life's sometimes funny,
But sometimes it's sad.

PART THREE
SOMETHING GOOD, SOMETHING BAD.

Talk about it

1. Finish this sentence: The funniest thing I ever saw was…
2. When you're sad, what do you do to feel better?

LESSON

9

Once Too Often

Look and answer

Tell what you see in the picture.

The boy who...

It was a slow Friday afternoon and Fred was bored. He was tired of watching television, and he was too lazy to do anything else. His mother was still at work, his Dad was in town doing some shopping, and his sister Jenny, two years
5 younger, was playing baseball *outside*.[1] He could hear them laughing: that made him feel more bored. Fred was *all alone*[2] in the house, and he was *very bored indeed*.[3]

He opened a book, but closed it again. He looked at a magazine, but then threw it down. Nothing was interesting.
10 Just for something to do, he put his head out of the window and shouted "Help! Help!"

Jenny and her friends heard him. They stopped their game and *came running*[4] to see what was wrong. When Fred saw how he had fooled them, he laughed and laughed.
15 Jenny and her friends were angry with him.

"That was stupid, Fred!" she said.

But Fred just laughed even more. He'd played a great joke!

Soon he was bored again. The street was empty now. He decided he would try it again. He put his head out of the

[1] out of the house
[2] alone
[3] very, very bored
[4] ran

57

window and shouted "Help! Help!" He looked around.

This time two neighbors ran to help him. When they saw that nothing was wrong, they were angry with him, too.

"Now that was very stupid, young man," said Mr.
25 Hubley, the next door neighbor.

"Someday you'll really need help," said Mrs. Chung, the old lady who lived across the street, "and no one will believe you."

But Fred was delighted with his joke. He had fooled
30 everyone twice.

Next day, it happened again. Fred was alone in the house, and *as usual*,[5] he was very bored. He found some cigarettes and matches. Maybe he would try smoking. He put a cigarette in his mouth and lit it. As the dirty smoke went
35 into his mouth, he started to cough. He felt sick. He threw away the cigarette and ran to the bathroom.

The cigarette fell on the floor. When Fred came back, the rug was on fire. There were big yellow, red, and orange flames all around the room, and there was thick smoke
40 everywhere. In a few minutes the house was on fire.

Fred was scared. He really needed help this time. He ran out into the street and shouted "Help! Fire!"

Mr. Hubley was in his garden, but he didn't listen to Fred. Mrs. Chung was reading the newspaper at her back door,
45 but she didn't even look up. Nobody came, because nobody believed him; they *had been*[6] fooled once too often. And so, Fred's house burned *to the ground*.[7]

[5] the same as always

[6] were

[7] completely; to the earth

New words for reading

Nouns

joke(s)   funny game or story
  Fred thought his joke was very funny.

match(es)   **smoke**

Adjectives

bored   not interested
  Fred was feeling bored.

delighted   very happy
  He was delighted with his joke.

empty   with nothing in it
  The street was empty; nobody was there.

lazy   not wanting to work

  Fred was watching television because he was too lazy to go out.

thick   heavy

  Thick smoke was everywhere.

tired of   bored with

  I'm tired of playing this game.

Adverbs

once   one time

twice   two times

Verbs

to burn   to be in flames

  The house was burning.

to fool   to do something funny; to make a joke

  Fred fooled the neighbors twice.

Idioms and expressions

once too often   one time too many

  Fred played his joke **once too often.**

just for fun   only for fun; for no other reason

  Just for fun he shouted, ''Fire! Fire!''

on fire   with fire everywhere; burning

  ''Help! My dress is **on fire!**''

to play a joke   to fool; to do something for a laugh

  He'd **played a** great **joke.**

too lazy to do anything else   very lazy; only wanting to do one thing

  Fred was watching television because he was **too lazy to do anything else.**

Grammar

Past Perfect Tense

EXAMPLES:

He **had fooled** them.
He**'d played** a great joke!
He **had fooled** everyone twice.

When several things happen in the past, use the Past Perfect tense to tell which action came first.

1. *First:* Fred fooled Jenny and her friends.
2. *Next:* He saw how he did that.
3. *Then:* He laughed and laughed.

Put the actions in order in one sentence using the Past Perfect.

(2)   (1)   (3)

When Fred **saw** how he **had fooled** them, he **laughed** and **laughed**.

More irregular Simple Past forms

to find   He **found** matches in the kitchen.

to light   He **lit** a cigarette.

Exercises

9A True or false

Read these statements and then read the text again to find out whether they are true or false.

_____ 1. Fred's mother was at home.
_____ 2. Fred is Jenny's sister.
_____ 3. Jenny was delighted with Fred for playing the joke.
_____ 4. Fred started a fire.
_____ 5. The house burned to the ground.

9B What's the order?

Write these sentences in the correct order so that they tell the story of Fred. The first sentence is marked for you.

_____ a. But the third time he shouted, nobody came.
_____ b. He was so bored that he decided to play a joke.
__1__ c. Fred was alone at home, and he was bored.
_____ d. But this time, he *really* needed their help: the house was on fire.
_____ e. Twice he shouted "Help! Help!" from the window, and twice people came running.

9C Tell another story

Fred played his joke once too often. When he really needed help, nobody came. Do you know another story like this one? Tell it to your classmates.

LESSON

10

Gift of the Heart

Look and answer

Describe the person in each picture.

Think about it

One person will give the other a gift. Guess which one.

Felipe and Donna

Felipe was fifteen years old, and he was *small for his age.*[1] He was often very sad, but he did not know why. He liked to joke with his friends and make them laugh, but he still felt sad.

5   Sometimes Felipe would get headaches which left him feeling very tired and depressed. The only time he was happy was when he went after school to have an ice cream or soda at the restaurant on the corner. He went to see Donna, who worked there after school as a waitress.

[1] not as tall as most people his age.

62

¹⁰ Donna was fourteen. She had soft brown hair, clear blue eyes, and tiny brown freckles on her nose and cheeks. Felipe thought she was very pretty. He wanted so much to talk to her, but he was very shy. He could only say ''Hi!'' and ''How are you?''—nothing else. But he liked to be in ¹⁵ the restaurant where he could look at her, and see her happy smile.

Then one day Felipe learned that Donna was very sick. There was something wrong with her heart, and the doctors said she would not live for more than two months. Felipe ²⁰ was very upset. Donna was going to die and he could do nothing about it. Feeling helpless, he told his mother one day, ''if I die, give my heart to Donna.''

Very unexpectedly,[2] Felipe's headaches became much worse. One day he lay on his bed to rest. He closed his eyes, ²⁵ and never opened them again. Felipe was dead.

His mother remembered what he had said, and his heart was transplanted into Donna's chest. And Donna lived.

[2] nobody thought it was going to happen

New words for reading

Nouns

gift(s) a present; something you give
Felipe's gift to Donna was wonderful.
headache(s) pain in the head
Felipe often had bad headaches.
smile(s)

heart(s)
chest(s)
face(s)
cheek(s)
nose(s)
freckle(s)

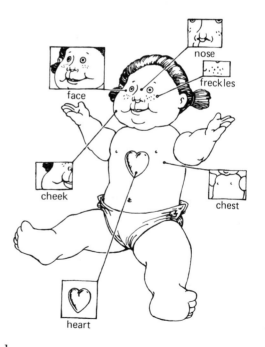

Adjectives

DESCRIBING HOW PEOPLE FEEL:

depressed	sad all the time
helpless	feeling that there is no help
shy	not liking to talk with new people
upset	unhappy, angry
worse	more bad than before

Verb

to transplant   to put inside another person or place

Felipe's heart was transplanted into Donna's chest.

Idioms and expressions

Felipe **would get** headaches.
>   Felipe often had headaches.

He liked **to make people laugh**.
>   Felipe made jokes; then people laughed. He liked this.

Grammar

Reported speech and thinking

Notice these examples of telling what people said or thought in the present and in the past.

Present:
The doctors **say** she **will** not **live** for more than two months.

Past:
The doctors **said** she **would** not **live** for more than two months.

Present:
Felipe **thinks** Donna **is** very pretty.
Felipe **thinks** Donna **is going to die** and he **can do** nothing.

Past:
Felipe **thought** Donna **was** very pretty.
Felipe **thought** Donna **was going to die** and he **could do** nothing.

More irregular Simple Past forms

to go   He **went** after school to have an ice cream.

to feel   He still **felt** sad.

to think   Felipe **thought** Donna was very pretty.

Exercises

10A Opposites

Happy is the opposite of sad. Read the text again to find the opposites of these words.

1.	to live	**4.**	big (2 words)
2.	right	**5.**	closed
3.	ugly	**6.**	well

10B True or false

Read these statements and then read the text again to find out whether they are true or false.

_____ **1.** Felipe and Donna were both fifteen years old.
_____ **2.** Felipe did not want to talk to Donna.
_____ **3.** Donna had something wrong with her heart.
_____ **4.** The doctors said that Felipe was dying.
_____ **5.** Felipe's heart was transplanted into Donna's chest.

10C New words

Make a summary of the story of Felipe and Donna. Choose from the words in **bold type**.

transplanted	**school**	**heart**	**shy**	**die**
restaurant	**upset**	**happy**	**depressed**	

Felipe was often very _____ but he was always

_____ when he was near Donna. He used to go to the

_____ where she worked after _____, just to be near

her. He wanted so much to talk to her, but he was too _____

to say very much.

When Donna became ill, Felipe was terribly _____; he

told his mother, "If I _____, give my _____ to

Donna."

Felipe died soon after that and his heart was _____ into

Donna's chest. It was a wonderful gift.

10D Talk about it

Do you think it is good to transplant hearts? Tell why or why not.

LESSON

My Favorite Star

What about *you*?

1. Who is your favorite star?
2. Is your favorite star on TV, in the movies, or both?
3. What is special about him or her?

They're Special!

My favorite movie star *knows how to*[1] fight and he *has a lot of muscles*.[2] All his movies have a lot of action, fights, and killings.

Dimitri

[1] can
[2] is strong
[3] looks and acts different
[4] boys; men

5 My favorite movie star *has a special style*.[3] She is not like any other movie star. Her clothes are very different, and her songs and dances are very exciting. She is a very different kind of star.

Ingrid

10 My favorite TV star is Goofy. He's not a person. He's a dog. I've always liked to watch cartoons about Mickey Mouse and Goofy. Goofy acts like a man. He's a very funny dog. I really like the situations he gets into and how he gets out of them. I still watch cartoons and I like them. You
15 know, there's always a part of you that is a child. Don't you think?

Ramon

My favorite rock star is Johnny D. He's unbelievable! He's incredibly handsome, but so are lots of other guys.[4] Sure, he
20 looks great in leather and denim, but that's not so unusual.

66

What makes Johnny special is—he's cool! He knows where he's going, and he's going in style. He's tough and he's tender. All my girlfriends agree: he's perfect—a perfect 10!

Joanna

[5] Post Scriptum What you forgot to write in the letter

Letter to Debbie

Dear Debbie,

Hi! How are you? I'm your biggest, I mean *biggest* fan. I would love to meet you. I see your concerts and I get all your tapes and videotapes. I have my room filled with your
[5] posters. My girlfriend likes you too, but she is a little mad, because when you come on TV I pay more attention to you than her. Tell the drummer in your band that I say hi. He's the person I like best after you. No one can take your place, not even my girlfriend. In my dreams I wish that I could talk
[10] to you in person and be close friends. It is only a dream, but sometimes dreams come true. I hope this one comes true!

Love always,
Your friend,
Paul

[15]

P.S.[5] Please write to me.

New words for reading

Nouns

> **band(s)**   a group of people who play music
>
>   *My brother plays in a band on Saturday nights.*
>
> **cartoon(s)**

> **clothes**   things a person wears, like a shirt, shoes
>
> **concert**   music played or sung for other people
>
>   *Are you going to the rock concert tonight?*
>
> **denim**   cotton cloth
>
>   *Blue jeans are made from denim.*
>
> **drummer(s)**   person who plays music on a drum
>
> **fan(s)**   person who really likes a star
>
> **leather**   clothes made from the skin of animals, usually jackets, shoes, or pants
>
> **movie(s)**   moving picture; film
>
>   *I liked that movie. (the thing)*
>
> **the movies**   cinema
>
>   *Do you want to go to the movies? (the place)*
>
> **movie star(s)**   popular movie actor or actress
>
> **rock (rock and roll)**   a kind of popular music

tape(s)

videotape(s)

MORE NOUNS FROM VERBS:

to act   I love the **action** in her movies.
to dance   The **dances** are very exciting.
to fight   All his movies have a lot of **fights**.
to kill   They also have a lot of **killings**.

Adjectives

cool   wonderful; popular; with an easy style
mad   angry
perfect   nothing is wrong
special   different and wonderful
tender   kind
tough   strong
unusual   not usual; special

Idioms and expressions

to get into/out of situations   to have problems and then find the solution
I like the way Goofy **gets into difficult situations** and how he **gets out of them**.

a perfect 10   If zero is terrible, and 5 is okay, then 10 is perfect.
In some games, **a perfect 10** is the best.

to pay attention to   to listen to and watch carefully
Our teacher is always saying, "**Pay attention to** the lesson!"

to take someone's place   to mean the same, to be as important
I'll always love you best. No one will ever **take your place**.

Grammar

Verbs with "like"

to like   I **like** Goofy. He's my favorite TV star.
to be like   Sam **is like** Andy. They wear the same clothes.
            Linda **is not like** Lisa. Lisa can sing, but Linda can't.
to act like   Goofy is a cartoon dog, but he **acts like** a man.
to like to + verb   I'm eighteen and I still **like to watch** cartoons.

Exercises

11A New words

Fill in the blanks. Choose from the words in **bold type**.

knows how to   **has a lot of muscles**   **style**   **cool**
a different kind   **situations**   **gets into**   **gets out of**

1. My favorite movie star is tough and he _____.

2. Well, my favorite movie star isn't strong, but she really _____ sing.

3. This star _____ many funny _____, and then _____

    them.

4. Johnny D. has a very different _____. He's not like any other star.

5. My sister likes _____ of movie star.

6. He's really _____.

11B Talk about it

Get together with one or two classmates. Find out who their favorite stars are, and why.

11C Write a letter

Write a short letter to your favorite TV, movie, or rock star. Be sure to tell why you like him or her.

LESSON

12

For Fun!

Tongue twisters

1. Say this three times quickly: THE FAT CAT SAT ON A MAT.
2. Now say *this* three times quickly: SHE SELLS SEASHELLS BY THE SEASHORE.

[1] Arab leader

3. Try this one: THE SIXTH *SHEIK'S*[1] SIXTH SHEEP IS SICK.
4. How about: RUBBER BABY-BUGGY BUMPERS

5. Or: TOY BOAT
6. Or: RED LEATHER, YELLOW LEATHER

Rhymes

Fuzzy[2] *Wuzzy*
Fuzzy Wuzzy was a bear.
A bear was Fuzzy Wuzzy.
When Fuzzy Wuzzy *lost*[3] his hair
He wasn't fuzzy, *wuzzy?*[4]

[2] with hair
[3] had no more
[4] "was he?"
[5] "mister"
[6]

[7] to get even
[8] same

The Mr.[5] *who kr. sr.*
She *frowned*[6] and called him Mr.
When, just for fun, he kr.
And so, *for spite,*[7]
That *very*[8] night
This Mr. kr. sr.

New words for reading

Nouns

rhyme(s)   poems with rhyming words
tongue twister(s)   words that are difficult to
                      pronounce quickly;

Tongue twisters make your tongue feel funny!

Verb

to rhyme   to have the same sound at the end (of words)
  "Cat" and "mat" rhyme.

Rhyming

The last word of each line of a rhyme is a rhyming word. Sometimes other words in a rhyme sound the same, too:

fuzzy/wuzzy
bear/hair
Mr. (**mister**)/kr. (**kissed her**)/ sr. (**sister**)
spite/night

Exercises

12A Matching rhyming words

Match the rhyming words in the columns below.

_____	**1.**	fuzzy	**a.**	hair
_____	**2.**	spite	**b.**	wuzzy
_____	**3.**	bear	**c.**	night
_____	**4.**	Mr.	**d.**	twister
_____	**5.**	rhyme	**e.**	time

12B Rhyming game

Make lists of all the words you know that rhyme with the letters below. Then use the lists to play a game with the class. When one person calls out a word, raise your hand and call out a rhyming word from your list. After that, think of other rhyming letters and make more words.

1. -at (at; bat; cat)
2. -et (bet; met)
3. -ing (sing; thing)
4. -ore (more; store)
5. -ug (bug; dug)
6. -ake (take; cake)

12C Make your own rhyme

Make a rhyme of your own. Choose from your favorite rhyming words from the text, from 12B or below. Use your own rhyming words, if you like.

EXAMPLES:

The cat was in a fight.
I heard it last night.

I wish I knew
Who has my blue shoe.

cat	fight	blue
rat	night	who
sat	light	shoe
hat	right	too

12D Make your own tongue twisters

Think of some combinations of words that are difficult, but fun, to pronounce. Share them with the class.

PART FOUR
DISASTER!

The weather can be violent, and the earth can move suddenly. Things can go wrong. Sometimes it's serious, sometimes not.

Talk about it

Describe what you see in the pictures.

Paul Benoit

LESSON

The Day the Mountain Moved

Look and answer

1. Tell what you see in the picture.
2. What do you think has happened?

Avalanche at Aberfan

Glynis opened her eyes slowly. What had happened?
From the window she could see an ambulance and two
black cars driving fast out of the *car park*[1] and away along
the road up the valley. It was raining hard. The day was
5 dark. And the green mountains and the black *coal tips*[2]
looked just the same. Why was she *in hospital*?[3]

[1] parking lot (U.S.)

[2]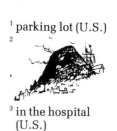

[3] in the hospital
(U.S.)

79

She closed her eyes again and began to think. She thought back to the morning before she went to school. She saw the kitchen table with a blue tablecloth, a *packet*[4] of
10 cornflakes, a piece of toast and *marmalade*,[5] and her homework, still not finished.

"*I'm off*,"[6] said her Dad as he closed the door behind him. Her father worked *down the coal mine*,[7] just outside the village.

15 "Come on, Glynis. *Shift yourself!*"[8] You'll be late," said her *Mam*.[9]

Glynis finished her *tea*,[10] picked up her school bag, and set off down the *steep*[11] mountain road towards the school. She *was* late, but still she didn't hurry. It was only five
20 minutes. And anyway, today was a *half-holiday*:[12] you didn't study much on a half-holiday.

[4] box (U.S.)
[5] kind of jam
[6] I'm leaving
[7] down in the coal mine (U.S.)
[8] Hurry!
[9] mother
[10] The British drink tea at any time of day
[11]

[12] holiday for half a day, either the morning or the afternoon
[13] wet and dirty
[14] like hills
[15] dirty
[16] side of the mountain

It had been raining a lot and everything was very *muddy*.[13] The coal-tips—huge *heaps*[14] of black earth, as big as the mountains themselves—looked wet and *foul*.[15] As she
25 looked up Glynis could see some water pouring down the side of one of the tips, washing grey stones and black earth away down the *mountainside*.[16]

She wondered whether the rain could wash all the tips
away from the valley. She looked up toward the mountains
30 and tried to imagine them without the coal tips, green and
fresh as they were before the mines opened two hundred
years ago. Then she looked down toward the village; the
chapel,[17] the school, and all the houses stood *tight*[18] together, and the big ugly coal tips looked down at them from
35 above.

As Glynis stood *gazing*[19] at the grey roofs of the village,
she heard a distant rumble. The rumble became a roar, as
down the mountain a great *wave*[20] of black earth came
rolling, crashing and smashing and swallowing everything
40 in its path. It was moving angrily towards the village,
towards the houses where people were finishing breakfast,
towards the shops which were just opening for the day,
towards the school where everyone was getting ready for
the half-holiday.

45 ''No!'' she screamed. ''No! NO-O-O-O!''. She ran towards
the village. She had to tell everyone to get out. They would
be buried alive. She ran faster. She was so afraid. More
waves of black were crashing toward the village. She
screamed again. She could *hardly*[21] breathe.

50 The roar was *deafening*[22] as she ran across the school
playground. As she looked up, the great wet black wave
appeared over the roof of the school. And then, nothing.

''The mountain is moving!'' Glynis cried.

''Yes, little one,'' said the nurse, speaking in *Welsh*.[23] ''It's
55 over now. There, there.''

''And the village?...and the school?'' asked Glynis.

''Sleep, now, little one. It's over.''

Historical Note
60 On Friday, 21 October 1966 at 9:15 A.M., an avalanche of
coal waste[24] slid from the mountain where it had sat, on to
the village of Aberfan, Wales. One of the buildings that it
covered was the primary school, where most of the children
were already in class.

65 More than two hundred people died in the avalanche.
Most of them were children between the ages of four and
eleven.

[17] church
[18] near
[19] looking for a long time
[20] usually, water moving on the ocean; here: earth moving down the mountainside
[21] almost not
[22] very, very loud
[23] language spoken in Wales
[24] what is thrown away after the coal is mined

New words for reading

Nouns

ambulance(s)   special truck to carry sick or hurt people

avalanche(s)   rocks, dirt, or snow falling down a mountain

coal   black rock that can be burned

disaster(s)   something bad that happens, often a terrible accident

earth   rocks and dirt
  Black earth came down the mountain.

mine(s)   place under the earth where people dig out coal or other rocks

rumble(s)   low noise from far away
  Glynis heard a distant rumble.

valley(s)   low land between mountains

Verbs

to be buried   to be covered with earth
  They would be buried alive.

to crash   to fall hard and with a loud noise
  A great wave of black earth came crashing down.

to roll   to turn
  The rocks rolled down the mountain.

to set off (set off)   to leave
  Glynis set off to school.

to slide (slid)   to move over something wet
  The earth slid down the mountain.

to smash   to break
  The avalanche smashed everything in its path.

to swallow   usually, to eat or drink; here: to cover over
  The earth swallowed everything in its path.

Grammar

Conditional with ''would'' or ''could''

If the avalanche **comes**, it **will bury** them alive.
If the avalanche **came**, it **would bury** them alive.
If the avalanche **came**, they **would be buried** alive.

She **wonders** whether the rain **can wash** all the tips away.
She **wondered** whether the rain **could wash** all the tips away.

Progressive Tenses:

Compare the Progressive Tenses.

Present Progressive:
It **is raining** now.
They **are finishing**.

Past Progressive:
It **was raining** last night.
They **were finishing**.

Present Perfect Progressive:
It **has been raining** all day.

Past Perfect Progressive:
It **had been raining** before the avalanche.

Exercises

13A True or false

Read these statements and then read the text again to find out whether they are true or false.

1.   Glynis was late for school.
2.   Her father was a miner.
3.   The coal tips had been on the mountain for more than a hundred years.
4.   When she saw the coal tip move, Glynis ran back home.

13B What's the order?

Put these sentences in order. Start with the thing that happened *first*, then put what happened *next* and so on. The last one has been marked for you.

_____ **a.**   Glynis looks down at the village.
_____ **b.**   Glynis finishes her tea.
__5__ **c.**   Glynis finds herself in the hospital.
_____ **d.**   Glynis sees the coal tip start to move.
_____ **e.**   Glynis runs to tell people in the village.

13C Talk about it

Glynis had to stay in the hospital for a long time. She was not badly hurt, but she was very upset.

1.   What do you think she thought about?
2.   What would you have done in her situation?
3.   What could you say to someone who has had a terrible experience?

13D Write about it

Write a letter to Glynis in the hospital.

From Bad to Worse

a. a bird

b. a cat

c. a dog

d. a fly

e. a horse

f. a spider

Look and answer

Look at the pictures. Match the words at the side with the pictures.

Think about it

1. Do people eat these animals?
2. Which of these animals do people almost never eat?

An Old Folk Song

There was an old woman who swallowed a fly.
I don't know why she swallowed a fly.
Perhaps she'll die.

There was an old woman who swallowed a spider
⁵ that *wriggled*[1] and wriggled and *tickled*[2] inside her.
She swallowed the spider to catch the fly,
but I don't know why she swallowed the fly.
Perhaps she'll die.

There was an old woman who swallowed a bird.
¹⁰ How absurd to swallow a bird!
She swallowed the bird to catch the spider
that wriggled and wriggled and tickled inside her.
She swallowed the spider to catch the fly,
but I don't know why she swallowed the fly.
¹⁵ Perhaps she'll die.

There was an old woman who swallowed a cat.
Fancy that! She swallowed a cat!
She swallowed the cat to catch the bird.
She swallowed the bird to catch the spider
²⁰ that wriggled and wriggled and tickled inside her.
She swallowed the spider to catch the fly,
but I don't know why she swallowed the fly.
Perhaps she'll die.

There was an old woman who swallowed a dog.
²⁵ What a *hog!*[3] She swallowed a dog.
She swallowed the dog to catch the cat.
She swallowed the cat to catch the bird.
She swallowed the bird to catch the spider
that wriggled and wriggled and tickled inside her.
³⁰ She swallowed the spider to catch the fly,
but I don't know why she swallowed the fly.
Perhaps she'll die.

There was an old woman who swallowed a horse.
She's dead, of course!

[1] moved fast

[2] touched and made her laugh
[3] pig

▸   ᵣor reading

ₐ) familiar song

Idioms and expressions

How absurd!   That's really stupid!
Fancy that!   Imagine that!
(To go) from bad to worse   To start with something bad and go to something worse
Of course!   It must be true!
What a hog!   That person is really like a pig! (eats too much)

Repeating rhymes

This folk song starts with one action, adds another action, then repeats. So, it's fun to sing and easy to remember. Notice the rhyming words:

fly/die
spider/inside her
bird/absurd
cat/that
hog/dog
horse/course

Grammar

Long sentences made from short sentences

Who and **that** are often used.

Short:
There was an old woman.
She swallowed a spider.
It wriggled…inside her.

Long:
There was an old woman **who** swallowed a spider **that** wriggled…inside her.

Question words like **why (when, where, what, who, how)** are often used.

Short:
She swallowed a fly.
Why did she?
I don't know.

Long: I don't know **why** she swallowed a fly.

Exercises

14A New words

Tell the story again. Choose from the words in **bold type**.

horse	**bird**	**woman**	**catch**	**fly**
spider	**dies**	**swallows**	**dog**	**cat**

   The song is about an old woman who _____ a _____,

and then swallows lots of other animals to try to _____ the fly. First

she swallows a _____, then a _____, then a

_____, then a _____, and finally a _____.

After she swallows the horse, she _____.

14B Read and remember

Get together with a partner. Read the song again and try to remember the words without looking at the text.

14C Talk about it

Are there any other funny songs like this in your language? Do you know one? Talk to your classmates about it.

The White Disaster

What about *you*?

1. Do you remember some very bad weather?
2. When did it happen?
3. What happened?
4. What did you do?

Boston Globe. Photo by David L. Ryan.

Gravely-Clemmons

The Great Blizzard of '78

November, 1977

U.S. Predicts Mild Winter

WASHINGTON, D.C.—Dr. Donald L. Gilman, *director*[1] of the National Weather Service said this winter is going to be warm. He also predicted that the winter will be wetter than *normal*.[2] "But weather forecasting is *risky business*,"[3] he added.

[1] manager; directs the work of others
[2] usual
[3] a difficult and unsure job
[4] we think it will snow

Sunday, February 5, 1978

Big Storm on the Way

BOSTON, MASSACHUSETTS—*Snow is expected*[4] tonight and Monday.

Boston Herald. Photo by Ted Fitzgerald.

Boston Herald. Photo by R. Sennott.

Monday, February 6, and Tuesday, February 7, 1978

Blizzard of '78

BOSTON—The worst storm *of the century*,[5] and perhaps in all *recorded*[6] weather history struck the New England area Monday and Tuesday. The blizzard lasted more than 32 hours. It dropped 27 inches of snow in Boston and killed 54 people in New England. The snow buried 3,500 cars and trucks on the highway. Ten thousand people are *homeless*.[7] *Damage*[8] was at least one billion dollars.

[5] since 1900
[6] written
[7] without homes
[8] the value of what was broken or destroyed
[9] taking away

Wednesday, February 8, 1978

The Big Dig

BOSTON—The sun came out today and an army of snow fighters of all ages are at work. Nine thousand workers and more than 3,000 snowplows and trucks are *removing*[9] the snow from the roads, rescuing people, and delivering food, medicine, and heating oil. The biggest problem is not the snow, but the flooding.

More problems: 100,000 people in Boston have no electricity—no light, no heat, no TV!

Boston Herald.

Boston Herald. Photo by Ted Fitzgerald.

Storm Stories

1. The window at Alexander's Pizza was blown out by ninety-mile-per-hour winds.

2. Police can't get to work. A lot of snowplows *are stuck*[10] in fifteen-foot drifts.

3. Some streets near the sea are under ten feet of water. There is serious flooding because of high tides. Boats have rescued hundreds from their homes. There are at least ten thousand homeless.

4. There were few *emergencies*[11] in Concord, Massachusetts, but the police did "*rush*"[12] Mrs. Emily Drop to Emerson Hospital (at 5 miles per hour) for the birth of her baby girl. The Drops have named their daughter Snow.

5. Eleven thousand people at a *hockey*[13] game in Boston could not go home Monday night, February 6. They were at the stadium until noon on February 8.

6. "Twice a day I thought I was going to die," said Anthony Chiarella of Revere, a town on the ocean. "We froze and we *prayed*,[14] and that's all we did between tides."

7. A little dog name Fufu was inside a snowdrift for eleven days. When he came out he bit his owner on the finger.

8. Dr. Buzz Congram skied to his hospital in downtown Boston yesterday. That night he skied across the bridge to Cambridge to a party. "The snow is so clean! It was great fun!" said Dr. Congram.

9. "Our neighbors were wonderful during the storm," said Mrs. Al Lowe. "We're almost eighty years old, and we couldn't get out to the supermarket. My husband needed more medicine. The young people next door walked to the store for us, and called us on the phone many times."

10. "It's the most fun I ever had—and no school for a whole week," declared Tom Reilly, twelve years old. "We built three fifteen-foot snowmen in our front yard. The TV people came, and we were on the six o'clock news."

[10] can't move
[11] situations when help is needed quickly
[12] "take quickly" (not really)
[13] sport played on ice
[14] asked God for help

Boston Herald. Photo by Angela Kaloventzos.

New words for reading

Nouns

blizzard(s)   very bad snowstorm with heavy wind
drift(s)   small hill of snow made by the wind
flooding   high water in the streets, inside houses
forecasting   telling the future weather
tide(s)   water level on the coast that rises and falls every six hours

NOUNS WITH "**SNOW**":
snowman(men)   man built of snow
snowplow(s)   special truck for removing snow

Measurements

inch(es)

foot (feet)   1 foot = 12 inches

mile(s) per hour   how fast something can go in one hour

The wind was blowing 50 miles per hour.

Adjectives

mild   warm
worst   the most bad

Verbs

to predict   to tell the future
to rescue   to save; to help someone get out of a bad situation

Grammar

More Irregular Past forms

to bite   Fufu **bit** his owner on the finger.
to blow   The window at Alexander's Pizza **was blown** out.
to build   We **built** three fifteen-foot snowmen in our front yard.
to freeze   It was so cold our feet almost **froze**.
to strike   The worst storm of the century **struck** Monday.

Exercises

15A Ask and answer

Using the information below, make questions, then answer them. Read the stories again if necessary.

EXAMPLES:

a.   Dr. Donald Gilman/who
     Q: Who is Dr. Donald Gilman?
     A: (He's the) director of the National Weather Service.

b.   predict/what
     Q: What did Dr. Gilman predict?
     A: (He predicted) a warm (mild) winter, wetter than normal.

1. big storm on the way/when
2. worst storm of the century/where
3. the blizzard/how long
4. snow/how much
5. people killed/how many
6. cars and trucks/how many
7. homeless people/how many
8. cost of the damage/how much
9. biggest problem/what

15B Act it out

After you have made your list of questions and answers, work with a partner. One person is asking the questions, like a reporter, and the other is answering them.

15C Talk about it

What would you do if you heard that there was a big storm, like the blizzard of '78, and that there was no school, no driving, and the stores were closed? Match the phrases on the left with the sentences on the right. There may be more than one good answer. After you have finished, talk about your answers with a classmate.

_____ 1. No school for one week   **a.** Use the telephone.

_____ 2. No mail   **b.** Stay with friends.

_____ 3. No electricity   **c.** Walk, ski, or ride a horse.

_____ 4. No driving   **d.** Build a snowman.

_____ 5. No food in stores   **e.** Use a flashlight or oil lamp.

_____ 6. No house   **f.** Wear a coat and gloves.

_____ 7. No heat   **g.** Stay home and have fun.

_____ 8. No buses, trains, taxis, planes   **h.** Eat what you have in the house.

15D Match the stories and headlines (titles)

Match each of the following headlines with one of the Storm Stories on page 92. Use the number of the story.

_____ **a.** DOG BITES MAN
_____ **b.** THE SKIING DOCTOR
_____ **c.** STORM TIDES SCARE REVERE MAN
_____ **d.** BLIZZARD BRINGS MISS ''SNOW DROP''
_____ **e.** WATER, WATER EVERYWHERE NEAR OCEAN
_____ **f.** GOOD NEIGHBORS
_____ **g.** THE REILLYS' REALLY BIG SNOWMEN
_____ **h.** POLICE CAN'T WORK MONDAY
_____ **i.** ELEVEN THOUSAND STUCK 30 HOURS AT HOCKEY GAME!
_____ **j.** STORM BLOWS OUT WINDOW

15E Write about it

Imagine you were in the Blizzard of '78. Write about what happened to you and your family during the storm.

The *Titanic*

Talk about it

1. Look at the picture and describe it.
2. What have you heard about the *Titanic*?

Culver Pictures

About the *Titanic*

On the night of April 14, 1912, the British steamship *Titanic* hit an iceberg in the North Atlantic. The ship sank and 1,503 people lost their lives. A few of the survivors, who were children then, still remember that disastrous
5 shipwreck. This song is another way people remember that terrible night, and *pass along*[1] the story to their children.

[1] tell

"The Ship *Titanic*" (a camp song)

Oh, they built the ship Ti-ta-nic, to sail the o-cean blue, And they thought they had a ship that the water would never *leak through*, But *twas* on her *maid-en trip* that an ice-berg hit the ship, It was sad when that great ship went down

Chorus It was sad; oh, it was sad; It was sad when that great ship went down, to the bottom of the ____ Hus-bands and wives, lit-tle chil-dren lost their lives, It was sad when that great ship went down.

Oh, they built the ship *Titanic*, to sail the ocean blue,
And they thought they had a ship that the water would
    never *leak through*,[2]
But 'twas[3] on her *maiden*[4] trip that an iceberg hit the ship,
It was sad when that great ship went down.

    It was sad; oh, it was sad;
    It was sad when that great ship went down,
        to the bottom of the ____[5]
    Husbands and wives, little children lost their lives,
    It was sad when that great ship went down.

[2] come into
[3] it was
[4] first
[5] sea

New words for reading

Nouns

iceberg(s)   mountain of ice in the ocean.
shipwreck(s)   when a ship has an accident
steamship(s)   ship that runs by energy from steam
survivor(s)   person who does not die in an accident or disaster

Adjective

disastrous   terrible; full of disaster

Grammar

More Irregular Past forms

to lose...life(lives)   to die

  Husbands and wives, little children lost their lives.

to sink   to go down in the water

  The Titanic sank on April 14, 1912.

Exercises

16A Ask and answer

Find the answers to the following questions.
1. What was the name of the steamship?
2. What country owned it?
3. Where did it sink?
4. Why did it go down?
5. How many people lost their lives?

16B Sing about it

Learn to sing the song with your classmates.

16C Talk about it

The Blizzard of 1978 was a disaster and so was the avalanche in Wales in 1966. The *Titanic* disaster took the most lives. Talk about these three disasters. How were they the same and how were they different? Why did each one happen?

16D Write about it

Imagine you are being rescued from a disaster. You can save three things from your house. What would they be, and why would you save them?

PART FIVE
TELL ME A STORY

ONCE UPON A TIME
many years ago, in a far
... there lived a king.

A question:

Does a spider have six or eight legs?*

A riddle:

What can go up a chimney down, but can't go down a chimney up?**

Do you know any riddles? Share them with your classmates.

* eight.
** an umbrella

17

What is a bird?

Look at the animal pictures and their names.

bat

platypus

chicken

rooster

ostrich

1. Which ones can fly?
2. Which ones can *lay eggs?*[1]
3. Which ones are birds?

A Hot Day by the River

It was a hot day by the river. Annie sat *in the shade*[2] of a big tree reading her book. Her big brother Bill had fallen asleep on the riverbank, his big hat over his face. Everything was quiet; everything was peaceful; everything was
5 hot.

"Bill," said Annie, looking up from her book, "what's a bird?"

From under his hat, Bill *grunted*[3] "Huh?"

"I mean," said Annie, "is a bird an animal?"

[1] make eggs

[2] in the cool area; out of the sun

[3] made a short, low noise, like a pig

10 Bill was still half asleep. "I guess so," he replied. "A bird's an animal that flies."

"So, is a bat a bird?" asked Annie. "You know, a bat like we have in the *barn*?"[4]

Bill was now awake. "No, Nannie." (Bill always called
15 his sister "Nannie.") "A bat's a mammal, like a mouse."

"But a bat's an animal that flies," said Annie. "How come it's not a bird?"

"Well," said Bill, pushing his hat from his face, "a bat doesn't lay eggs. A bird is an animal that lays eggs."
20 "Oh," said Annie, and returned to her book.

[4] place on a farm where animals are kept

It was still quiet, still peaceful, still hot, hot, hot. Bill was falling asleep again. Annie turned the page of her book.

"What about a platypus?" she asked suddenly.

"A what?" said Bill, who was half asleep again.

25 "A P-L-A-T-Y-P-U-S," said Annie, spelling out the word in case she had pronounced it wrong. "It says here in this book that a platypus lives in Australia, and it's a mammal, and it lays eggs. So how come a platypus isn't a bird?"

"Can it fly?" asked Bill.

30 Annie looked at her book again. "No," she replied.

"Then I guess it isn't a bird if it can't fly," said Bill.

"But ostriches are birds, and they can't fly," said Annie, very puzzled.[5] "And chickens and roosters can't fly, and *they're* birds, aren't they?"

35 "They sure are, Nannie," said Bill from under his hat. "They sure are."

"So what *is* a bird?" asked Annie loudly.

"I guess I don't know, Nannie," said Bill sleepily.

Annie thought for a while. She looked up into the tree
40 where birds were sleeping in the heavy afternoon heat. A feather came falling slowly down, down, down, and fell on to the page of her open book.

"Feathers," said Annie, thoughtfully. "That's it! A bird has feathers. If it doesn't have feathers, then it's not a bird.
45 Isn't that right, Bill?"

But Bill was fast asleep on the riverbank, his big hat over his face. And everything was quiet; everything was peaceful; everything was hot, hot, hot.

[5] confused; not knowing what to think

New words for reading

Nouns

feather(s)

mouse (mice)

mammal(s)   animal with hair; the female gives milk to its young

riddle(s)   question or problem that needs a smart answer

Adjectives

OPPOSITES:

asleep   sleeping
awake   not sleeping

THE SAME:

half asleep
half awake

Adjectives and Adverbs

ADJECTIVE	ADVERB
peaceful feeling peace	**peacefully**
sleepy full of sleep	**sleepily**
sudden quick, unexpected	**suddenly**
thoughtful with much thought	**thoughtfully**

Idioms and expressions

fast asleep   completely asleep
How come?   Why?
They sure are.   They really are.

Grammar

More Irregular Past forms

to fall/to fall asleep

A feather **fell** on her book.
He had **fallen asleep** under the tree.

Exercises

17A True or false

Read these statements and then read the text again to find out whether they are true or false.

1. Bill said that a bat is a bird.
2. Bill said that a bat doesn't lay eggs.
3. It said in Annie's book that a platypus lays eggs.
4. Annie says that ostriches don't fly.
5. Annie thinks that all birds have feathers.

17B Contractions

Write the contraction of the words *in italics*. Check the text to see if you're right.

1. A *bird is* an animal that flies.   _____

2. A *bat is* a mammal.   _____

3. Ostriches *cannot* fly.   _____

4. But *they are* birds, *are they not*?   _____

5. I guess I *do not* know.   _____

6. *That is* it.   _____

7. If it *does not* have feathers, it *is not* a bird.   _____

8. *Is that not* right, Bill?   _____

17C Think about it

1. Annie says that all birds have feathers. Is that true? What do you think?
2. Can you think of any birds which *don't* have feathers?
3. Bill says that a bat is a mammal. Can you name ten more mammals in English?
4. What *is* a mammal?

LESSON

18

The Elephants and the Mice

Think about it

1. Can an elephant be a friend to a mouse?
2. Can cats and birds be friends?
3. What about horses and snakes?
4. What are some animals that *can* be friends?

Looking ahead

The story of the elephants and the mice is called a parable. A parable can teach something about life and how to be good. Notice how the writer "builds" the story. First, there is a beginning, or an introduction. Then, the main part tells the action. Finally, the story has an ending, or a conclusion. Read the following outline of the parts of a story, and look for the answers to the questions as you read about the mice and the elephants.

I.   **Introduction**
    a.   Where did the story happen?
    b.   When did it happen?
    c.   Who was in the story? (Who are the characters?)

II.   **Action**
    a.   What happened first?
    b.   Then what happened?
    c.   What was the biggest problem in the story?

III.   **Conclusion**
    a.   What was the solution to the problem in the story?
    b.   How did the story end?
    c.   What did you learn from the story?

How the Mighty Elephants And the Tiny Mice Became Friends

Introduction

Once upon a time in India there was a large, beautiful city *beside*[1] a lake. The people who lived there were rich and happy. But time passed, and this beautiful city *fell into* ruins.[2] All the people left, and they took all their animals with them.

Only the mice stayed. They began to live in all the old houses and *temples*.[3] The city beside the lake became a city of mice: many, many mice. Soon in every family there were grandfathers and grandmothers, fathers and mothers, husbands and wives, uncles and aunts, brothers and sisters and cousins, and lots and lots of baby mice.

They were all happy. They were always having feasts and festivals: spring festivals, harvest festivals, weddings, and all kinds of parties.

In a jungle far from the city there lived some elephants. Their king was wise and kind, and all the elephants loved him.

Action

The elephants were happy in the jungle, but there came a time of great trouble. There was no rain for several years and all the rivers dried up. The elephants went far and wide looking for water. Finally the king learned that there was a large lake on the other side of the ruined city. He led his

[1] next to
[2] became destroyed; fell down
[3] religious buildings; churches

25 elephants quickly through the ruined city, for they were very thirsty. They did not notice that the homes of thousands of tiny mice were being *crushed*[4] *beneath*[5] their feet. The mice were *in great sorrow.*[6] Many were homeless and hurt.

30 Then the rains came, and the elephants were ready to go back to the jungle. They would be coming through the old city again! The mice *called a meeting.*[7] What could they do to stop the elephants? They talked and talked, and then one wise old mouse said, "Let's go to the elephant king and ask

35 him not to pass through the city with his elephants."

Three brave mice went to the elephant king and told him their problem. The king said, "We will find some other path to our jungle. Go back to your city and live in peace."

A few years later the king of a nearby country needed

40 more elephants for his *army.*[8] He sent his men into the jungle to catch as many elephants as they could. They found the place where the king and all his elephants lived. They dug many deep pits and covered them with branches and leaves from the trees. They did this so that the

45 elephants would fall into the pits when they walked over them.

The elephants did fall in and were *trapped.*[9] The men brought *tame*[10] elephants and, using ropes, pulled the trapped elephants out and tied them to trees. The elephant

50 king was sad. How could they *escape?*[11] He tried and tried to think of a way to get free, but he could not. Suddenly he remembered the mice in the ruined city. Those mice had said they would help him.

The elephant king called to his queen, who was free. He

55 asked her to rush to the city of mice and tell them what had happened. She told them the story, and they said they would help their friends.

Conclusion

Then thousands and thousands of mice rushed to the

60 jungle where the elephants were tied to the trees. Many mice went to each elephant and with their strong teeth they cut through the ropes. The elephants were free! They were all very happy. The king and the queen of the elephants thanked the mice for setting them free so cleverly. One

65 mouse sat on the *trunk*[12] of the elephant king. "We are your friends," he said. "We are glad that we could help you."

[4] destroyed, smashed
[5] under
[6] very sad
[7] gathered together
[8] soldiers; fighters
[9] caught
[10] not wild; belonging to people
[11] run away; get free
[12] long nose

The mice and the elephants all sat down together to a great feast. "This is the happiest festival of all," said the mice. "It is a festival of friendship between mice and
70 elephants."

And from that day the mice and the elephants were close friends and they all lived happily ever after.

New words for reading

Nouns

feast(s)   big party with lots of food

festival(s)   a special event for an important reason: a special day, season, or person

friendship(s)   being friends

harvest(s)   when fruits and vegetables are picked

jungle(s)   forest in warm places

king(s)   male who rules or governs all the people in a country; husband of a queen

pit(s)   hole in the earth

queen(s)   female who rules or governs all the people in a country; wife of a king

NOUNS ABOUT READING STORIES:

action(s)/the action   what happens in a story

  The action begins when the elephants can't find water to drink.

character(s)   the people or animals in a story

  The characters in this story are mice and elephants.

conclusion(s)/the conclusion   the end of a story

The conclusion comes after the mice and elephants become friends.

introduction(s)/the introduction   the beginning of a story

We learn where the story happens and who the characters are in the introduction.

parable(s)   a simple story to teach a lesson

Adjectives

brave   not afraid
free   able to move; able to do what you want
mighty   large and strong
ruined   destroyed; broken
wise   knowing and understanding what is good or intelligent

Prepositions

beneath   under
far and wide   far
nearby   near

Idioms and expressions

Once upon a time   one time
   This is how many parables and old stories begin.

They all lived happily ever after.   Everyone was happy forever.
   This is how many old stories end.

Grammar

Simple and compound sentences

A simple sentence has only one subject and verb. **(This is a simple sentence.)**

A compound sentence has more than one subject and verb, and its parts are often connected by "and," "but," or "or." **(This is a compound sentence.)**

There are many, many compound sentences in the story. Notice how they are put together.

1. But time passed. *(simple sentence)*
2. This beautiful city fell into ruins. *(simple sentence)*
3. But time passed, and this beautiful city fell into ruins. *(compound sentence)*

Also:

1. The elephants were happy in the jungle.
2. There came a time of great trouble.
3. The elephants were happy in the jungle, but there came a time of great trouble.

"Could" and "would"

Could and **would** sometimes tell what can happen, probably will happen, or happened. Look for time clues in the sentence to determine if **could** or **would** tell about the future or the past.

They **would** be coming through the old city again! *(future)*
What **could** they do to stop the elephants? *(future)*
How **could** they escape? *(future)*
He sent his men to catch as many elephants as they **could**. *(past)*
They dug pits so that the elephants **would** fall into them. *(past)*

More irregular Simple Past forms

to bring   The men **brought** tame elephants out.
to cut   With their strong teeth they **cut** through the ropes.
to dig   They **dug** many deep pits.
to sit   One mouse **sat** on the trunk of the elephant king.

Exercises

18A Ask and answer

Look at the questions below. Read or listen to the story again and then write the answers to the questions.

Introduction:

1. Where does the story happen?
2. When does it happen?
3. Who are the important characters (animals and people)?

Action:

4. What is the first action?
5. What happens after the people and animals leave the city?
6. What happens next to the elephants?
7. How does this cause trouble for the mice?
8. How do the mice get help from the elephants?

9.   Why do the elephants need help later?
10. How do the mice help the elephants?

Conclusion:

11. How does the story end?

18B Think about it

1.   What is the story really about?
2.   Do you think this is only a story about animals? Tell why or why not, giving examples from the story.

18C Talk about it

What are some good ways to win friends? Make a list and discuss your ideas with the class.

18D Write about it

Choose one of the questions below and answer it in a few sentences.

1.   If you could be another animal, which would you be? Why?
2.   Think of your best friend. What animal would he or she be? Why?

LESSON

Anansi, the Spider Man

Think about it

1. Are some animals more intelligent than others?
2. Do you think that animals act like people?
3. How are people and animals the same? Different?

Talk about it

1. Did your parents or grandparents tell you stories?
2. What were some of your favorite stories when you were young?
3. Tell your favorite animal story.

About the Anansi Stories

Who was Anansi? He was a man and he was a spider. Anansi's home was in West Africa. From there long years ago thousands of men and women came to the islands of the Caribbean. They brought with them the stories that they
5   loved, the stories about clever Br'er¹ Anansi and his friends.

¹ Brother
² small house
³ many
⁴ because
⁵ going to
⁶ most important
⁷ any

Anansi and the Plantains

It was market day, but Anansi had no money. He sat at the door of his *cottage*² and watched Tiger and Cat, Dog and Goat, and *a host of*³ others hurrying to the market to buy and sell. He had nothing to sell, *for*⁴ he had not done any
10   work in his field. How was he *to*⁵ find food for his wife Crooky and for the children? *Above all*,⁶ how was he to find food for himself?

Soon Crooky came to the door and spoke to him. "You must go now, Anansi, and find something for us to eat. We
15   have nothing for lunch, nothing for dinner, and tomorrow the market is closed. What are we going to do without *a scrap of*⁷ food in the house?

"I am going out to work for some food," said Anansi. "Do not worry. Every day you have seen me go with nothing and
20   come home with something. You watch and see!"

Anansi walked about until noon and found nothing, so he lay down to sleep under the shade of a large mango tree. There he slept and waited until the sun began to go down. Then, in the cool of the evening, he set off for home. He
25   walked slowly, for he was ashamed to be going home empty-handed. He was asking himself what he was to do, and where he would find food for his children, when he came face to face with his old friend Rat going home with a large bunch of plantains on his head. The bunch was so big
30   and heavy that Brother Rat had to bend down almost to the earth to carry it.

Anansi's eyes shone when he saw the plantains, and he stopped to speak to his friend Rat.

"How are you, my friend Rat? I haven't seen you for a
35   very long time."

"Oh, I am staggering along, staggering along," said Rat. "And how are you—and the family?"

Anansi put on his longest face, so long that his chin

almost touched his toes. He groaned[8] and shook his head.
40 "Ah, Brother Rat," he said, "times are very hard. I can hardly find a thing to eat from one day to the next." At this,[9] tears[10] came into his eyes and he went on:

"I walked all yesterday. I have been walking all today and I haven't found a yam or a plantain." He glanced[11] for a
45 moment at the large bunch of plantains. "Ah, Br'er Rat, the children will have nothing but water for supper tonight."

"I am sorry to hear that," said Rat, "very sorry indeed. I know how I would feel if I had to go home to my wife and children without any food."
50 "Without even a plantain," said Anansi, and again he looked for a moment at the plantains.

Br'er Rat looked at the bunch of plantains, too. He put it on the ground and looked at it in silence.

Anansi said nothing, but he moved toward the plantains.
55 He could not take his eyes away from them, except to look quickly at Rat's face. Rat said nothing. Anansi said nothing. They both looked at the plantains.

Then at last Anansi spoke. "My friend," he said, "what a lovely bunch of plantains! Where did you get it in these
60 hard times?"

"It's all that I had left in my field, Anansi. This bunch must last[12] until the peas are ready, and they are not ready yet."

"But they will be ready soon," said Anansi, "they will be
65 ready soon. Brother Rat, give me one or two of the plantains. The children have eaten nothing, and they have only water for supper."

"All right, Anansi," said Rat. "Just wait a minute." Rat counted all the plantains carefully and then said,
70 "Well, perhaps, Br'er Anansi, perhaps!" Then he counted them again and finally he broke off the four smallest plantains and gave them to Anansi.

"Thank you," said Anansi, "thank you, my good friend. But, Rat, it's four plantains; and there are five of us in the
75 family—my wife, the three children, and myself."

Rat took no notice of this. He only said, "Help me to put this bunch of plantains on my head, Br'er Anansi, and do not try to break off any more."

So Anansi had to help Rat to put the bunch of plantains
80 back on his head. Rat went off, walking slowly because of the weight of the bunch. Then Anansi set off for his home.

[8] made a low, unhappy noise
[9] when he heard this
[10] water
[11] looked
[12] be enough; not be all gone

He could walk quickly because the four plantains were not *a heavy burden.*[13] When he got to his home he handed the four plantains to Crooky, his wife, and told her to roast

[85] them. He went outside and sat down in the shade of the mango tree until Crooky called out to say that the plantains were ready.

Anansi went back inside. There were four plantains, *nicely*[14] roasted. He took up one and gave it to the girl. He

[90] gave one each to the two boys. He gave the biggest plantain to his wife. After that he sat down empty-handed and very, very sad looking, and his wife said to him, "Don't you want some of the plantains?"

"No," said Anansi, *with a deep sigh.*[15] "There are only

[95] enough for four of us. I'm hungry, too, because I haven't had anything to eat; but there are just enough for you."

The little child asked, "Aren't you hungry, Papa?"

"Yes, my child, I am hungry, but you are too little. You cannot find food for yourselves. It's better for me to be

[100] hungry. I'm happy that your stomachs are filled."

"No, Papa," shouted the children, "you must have half of my plantain." They all broke their plantains in two, and each one gave Anansi a half. When Crooky saw what was happening she gave Anansi half of her plantain, too. So, in

[105] the end, Anansi got more than anyone, just as usual.

[13] too much to carry
[14] well
[15] breathing loudly and sadly

New words for reading

Nouns

Animals:

tiger(s)

goat(s)   small horned animal kept for its milk
rat(s)   animal like a large mouse

FRUITS AND VEGETABLES:

mango(es)
pea(s)

plantain(s)/bunch(es) of plantains
yam(s)

Adjectives

ashamed   feeling sorry for something you did
clever   intelligent

Verbs

to bend down

   Brother Rat had to bend down almost to the earth.

to roast   to cook in an oven or over a fire

Idioms and expressions

1. **empty-handed**   Anansi was ashamed to be going home **empty-handed**. He was carrying nothing.
2. **face to face**   He came **face to face** with his old friend Rat. They met.
3. **to stagger along**   "Oh, **I am staggering along**." "I'm okay, but it's difficult for me to walk, and life is hard."
4. **to put on a long face**   Anansi **put on his longest face**. He tried to look very, very sad.
5. **hard times**   "Where did you get that bunch of plantains in these **hard times**?" "There is little food or money, people are poor."
6. **to take no notice of**   "Rat **took no notice of** this." "Rat didn't seem to hear or see."

Grammar

Relative clauses

A relative clause is a part of a sentence. It has a subject and a verb, but it can't be a sentence alone. It tells more about the words that come before it. A relative clause often begins with **that.**

They brought with them the stories **that** they loved.
It's all **that** I had left in my field.

More Irregular Past forms

to eat	They **have eaten** nothing since yesterday.
	The children **ate** part of a plantain.
to shake	He groaned and **shook** his head.
to shine	Anansi's eyes **shone** when he saw the plantains.
to sleep	There he **slept** and waited for the sun to go down.

Exercises

19A Talk about it

Get together with one or two classmates and tell each other what you think.

1. Is Anansi a clever spider or not?
2. Do you think he loves his family?
3. Should clever people work hard or can they be lazy?
4. Is Rat a good friend to Anansi? A very good friend?
5. Do Anansi's children love him?
6. Is this story funny, sad, or both?
7. Which part is the funniest?
8. Which part is the saddest?

19B Write about it

What's the worst situation you've ever been in? How did you get out of it? Write a few sentences telling about your experience.

19C "Anansi and the Plantains: A Play"

Change the story into a short play. Go back to the story and write out all the conversations. Include all the characters. You may want to divide the story into parts, called "scenes." Then perform the play in class.

LESSON

The Right Question

Think about it

Here is a puzzle. Can you join these dots using only four straight lines without lifting your pen from the paper?

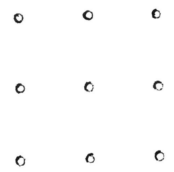

The answer is hidden in this lesson.

The Door of Iron and the Door of Gold

A traveler *found himself*[1] near a great wall as high as the sky and as long as the *horizon.*[2] There were two doors in the wall, one made of iron and one of gold.

The traveler remembered what he had been told. "Be-
5 yond[3] one of these doors," he said to himself, "lies a land of peace and happiness. Beyond the other lies a land of *misery and terror.*[4] How can I find out which is which?"

As he rode his horse closer to the doors he saw that there was a guard by each of them. "I will ask the guards," he
10 thought. "Surely they will tell me which door leads to the land of peace and happiness."

The guard of the iron door was a woman with a great

[1] was
[2] line where the earth seems to meet the sky
[3] on the other side of
[4] unhappiness and fear

121

sword in her hand. Her black hair was tied with a silver *cord*[5] and a *diamond*[6] *glistened*[7] in her nose. Her eyes looked
15 straight ahead and *her mouth was closed in a stern expression.*[8]

The guard of the golden door was a young man sitting on the back of a lion. His hair was as golden as the door he was

[5] rope
[6] expensive jewel that looks like glass
[7] shone
[8] her face had no smile

guarding, and he was dressed in a white *tunic*.[9] As he sat
astride[10] the lion, he held one hand behind his back; in his
other hand he held a book. His eyes were smiling, but his
lips were not.

[9] a long shirt

[10] on the back of
[11] or
[12] take
[13] went near to

On the wall between the doors was a message written in
black letters:

BELIEVE NOT WHAT IS IN THE HAND
NOR[11] WHAT IS IN THE EYES
FOR THERE IS ONE WHO TELLS THE TRUTH
BUT ONE TELLS ONLY LIES

"I must be careful," thought the traveler. "One of these
guards always tells the truth, but the other always tells lies.
How can I find out which is which? What question can I
ask?"

He thought for a long time, for many hours, for many
days. What question could he ask? How could he know
which guard was telling the truth? How could he find the
door to the land of peace and happiness?

He thought and thought, and at last he cried "Aha!" He
had found the right question, the question that would *lead*[12]
him to the land of peace and happiness.

He *approached*[13] the woman who guarded the iron door

[45] and asked her his question. *Raising*[14] her sword, she pointed to the golden door. Then he went to the young man sitting astride the lion and asked him the *same* question. Taking his hand from behind his back, the young man also pointed to the golden door.

[50]   "Then I must take the door of iron," thought the traveler. *Mounting*[15] his horse, he went through the door of iron, and entered the land of peace and happiness.

What question did the traveler ask the *guards*?[16]

[14] lifting
[15] getting on
[16] The question is hidden in the lesson.

New words for reading

Nouns

gold   yellow metal

guard(s)   person who watches over a place or person

iron   strong, dark metal

puzzle(s)   game that tests intelligence; a question that seems difficult to answer

silver   bright, light gray metal

sword(s)

traveler   person who travels

Adjectives

gold/golden
1. made of gold, a yellow metal
2. the color of gold

iron   made of iron, a strong, dark metal

silver
1. made of silver, a bright, light gray metal
2. the color of silver

Verbs and Nouns

to guard/guard(s)
The woman with the sword **was guarding** the iron door.
The other **guard** took care of the golden door.

Opposites

to tell the truth   to say true things
to tell lies   to say things that are not true

Grammar

More Irregular Past forms

to hold	He **held** one hand behind his back.
to ride	He **rode** his horse closer to the doors.
to write	There was a message **written** in black letters.

Exercises

20A Think about it

Read the description of the guards again. Which one tells the truth? Why do you think this?

20B Talk about it

The traveler's question got the *same* answer from both guards. What was the question?

20C Do another puzzle

Do you know any more puzzles? Share them with the class.

Indexes

New Words for Reading and Glossed Words

Note: Not all the words in the text appear in the Index. High-frequency words included in many basic multi-skill texts have not been included. For example, "dog" and "horse" appear in the text, but we assume most students are already familiar with these words. The past tense and past participles of irregular verbs appearing in the text are included in this Index. In some cases the designation of *expression* or *idiom* is arbitrary. In all cases the part of speech refers to the way a word is used in this text. The numbers refer to the lesson in which the word is glossed, introduced in the *New words for reading* or in the *Grammar* section.

Abbreviations

abbr.	=	*abbreviation*	*pl.*	=	*plural*
adj.	=	*adjective*	*p.p.*	=	*past participle*
adv.	=	*adverb*	*prep.*	=	*preposition*
conj.	=	*conjunction*	*pron.*	=	*pronoun*
contr.	=	*contraction*	*rel. pron.*	=	*relative pronoun*
expr.	=	*expression*	*sing.*	=	*singular*
id.	=	*idiom*	*v.*	=	*verb*
interj.	=	*interjection*	*U.K.*	=	*United Kingdom*
n.	=	*noun*	*U.S.*	=	*United States*
p.	=	*past tense*			

Numbers refer to lesson numbers.

A

above: ____ all *id.* 19
absurd: How ____! *expr.* 14
act *v.* 11; to ____ like *v.* 11
action *n.* 11, 18
age: small for his ____ *expr.* 10
alive *adj.* 8
alone: all ____ *id.* 9
ambulance *n.* 13
American *adj.* 8
approached (to approach) *v.* 20
area *n.* 4, 6
army *n.* 18
as: ____ usual *id.* 9
ashamed *adj.* 19
ask *v.* 6
asleep *adj.* 17
astride *prep.* 20
ate: See eat
attention *n.* 11
Australian *adj.* 8
avalanche *n.* 13

awake *adj.* 17

B

baby-buggy: rubber ____
    bumpers 12
bad, worse, worst *adj.*; to go
    from ____ to worse *expr.*
    14
band *n.* 11
barn *n.* 17
bat *n.* 17
be: to ____ like *v.* 7, 11; was,
    were *p.* 6;
    been, *p.p.* 9
began: See begin
begin *v.*; began *p.* 6
behalf: on ____ of *id.* 5
believe *v.* 3
bend: to ____ down *v.* 19
beneath *prep.* 18
beside *prep.* 18
beyond *prep.* 20

big; bigger; biggest *adj.* 6, 7
billion *n.* 4
bite *v.*; bit *p.* 15
bit: See bite
blew: See blow
blizzard *n.* 15
blow *v*; blew *p.* 15
border *n.* 5
bored *adj.*; very ____ indeed
    expr. 9
brave *adj.* 18
Br'er *n.* 19
bring *v.*; brought *p.* 18
British *adj.* 8; the ____ *n.pl.* 2
brought: See bring
brush *v.* 8
build *v.*; built *p.* 15
built: See build
bumper(s): rubber baby–buggy
    ____ 12
bunch *n.* 19
burden *n.* 19
buried *adj.* 13

Index of Place Names

This Index notes the Lesson where place names first occur.

Map of the English-Speaking World

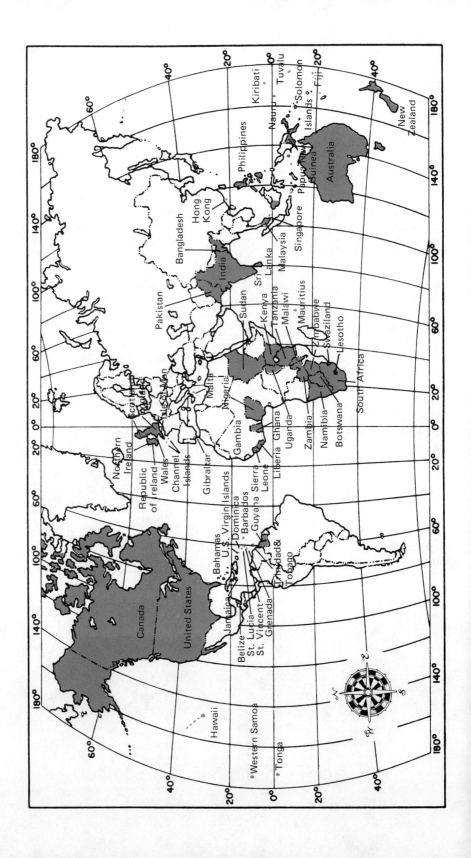

THE UNITED STATES OF AMERICA

MAINE
• Augusta

NEW HAMPSHIRE
VERMONT
• Montpelier

MASSACHUSETTS
• Concord
Boston •
RHODE ISLAND
Providence •
CONNECTICUT
Hartford •
New York City •

NEW YORK
Albany •

NEW JERSEY
Trenton •
DELAWARE
Dover •
Washington, D.C.
MARYLAND
Annapolis •

PENNSYLVANIA
Harrisburg •

WEST VIRGINIA
Charleston •

VIRGINIA
Richmond •

Raleigh •
NORTH CAROLINA

SOUTH CAROLINA
Columbia •

FLORIDA

OHIO
Columbus •

KENTUCKY
Frankfort •

TENNESSEE
Nashville •

GEORGIA
Atlanta •

ALABAMA
Montgomery •

Tallahassee •

MICHIGAN
Lansing •

INDIANA
Indianapolis •

ILLINOIS
Springfield •

WISCONSIN
Madison •

MINNESOTA
St. Paul •

IOWA
Des Moines •

MISSOURI
Jefferson City •

Mississippi River

ARKANSAS
Little Rock •

MISSISSIPPI
Jackson •

LOUISIANA
Baton Rouge •

NORTH DAKOTA
Bismarck •

SOUTH DAKOTA
Pierre •

NEBRASKA
Lincoln •

KANSAS
Topeka •

Missouri River

OKLAHOMA
• Oklahoma City

TEXAS
• Austin

MONTANA
Helena •

WYOMING
Cheyenne •

COLORADO
Denver •

NEW MEXICO
Sante Fe •

IDAHO
Boise •

UTAH
Salt Lake City •

ARIZONA
Phoenix •

WASHINGTON
Olympia •
Columbia River

OREGON
Salem •

NEVADA
Carson City •

CALIFORNIA
Sacramento •

HAWAII
Honolulu •

ALASKA
Juneau •